# We've Got to Stop Meeting Like This
## A memoir of missed connections

# PRAISE FOR

# We've Got to Stop Meeting Like This
## A memoir of missed connections

"This humorous, touching work brings inspiration and guidance to those facing the unexpected shadows life may cast. *Magical*."
*~Erin Byron, author Yoga for the Creative Soul*

"We all want to believe we can overcome loss or betrayal and Donna Ferris shows us her way. She did it!"
*~Jennifer Schelter, Radiant Retreat and Best of Philly Yoga Leader*

"Donna Ferris put her heart onto the pages of *We've Got to Stop Meeting Like This*, a vulnerable telling of three transformative years of her life told with openness. It's easy to see oneself at any stage of Donna's journey and to appreciate the strength it takes to survive loss in all its forms but most of all, to learn to love again."
*— Sharon Salzberg, author of Lovingkindness and Real Happiness*

"This memoir is a fun tale that weaves spiritual lessons into the fabric of life...Her example reminds me that I can be a normal person living extraordinarily."
*~Bob Butera, PhD, author of The Pure Heart of Yoga*

"In her kind, thoughtful entries, we come to understand that resilience and happiness truly do rest on the small, daily choices we make to heal, even as we stand on unsteady ground, and on our willingness to open to the new, and to what might be possible."
*~Maria Sirois, author of A Short Course in Happiness After Loss*

# We've got to Stop Meeting Like This

## A memoir of missed connections

by

DONNA Y. FERRIS

2022 MINICHANGE Publications Paperback Edition
Copyright ©2021 Donna Y. Ferris
All rights reserved.

ISBN 978-1-7367579-0-1 (paperback)
ISBN 978-1-7367579-1-8 (ebook)
ISBN 978-1-7367579-2-5 (audiobook)

Subjects: Memoir - Love & Loss, Love & Romance,
Grief & Bereavement

Book design by Amy Junod Placentra

Printed in the United States of America

*We've Got to Stop Meeting Like This* playlist can be found on Spotify
Webpage: www.minichangeyoga.com

"You have to work at your sense of conviction… Like someone lost in the forest, if you're not really convinced that there's a way out, you give up very easily. You run into a thicket here, a steep cliff there, and it just seems way too much. But if you're convinced there's got to be a way out, you've heard of other people who've made their way out, you think, 'It's got to be in here someplace.' You keep looking, looking, looking. And finally, you see how the other people made their way out: 'Oh. That was the path they took.'" ~Thanissaro Bhikkhu

# PROLOGUE

It's hard to hide from a husband. Especially while lying next to him in a ten-by-ten bedroom in a 900-square-foot condo on a Seven Mile Island off the coast of New Jersey. But that was my New Year's Day resolution. To be still like a rabbit, aware the hound is close yet oblivious.

The sound of a marimba phone alarm and a bright blue light filled the room.

"It's 6 a.m. Wakey wakey eggs and bakey."

I pulled the covers over my head. I hated when he said that. "Maybe we should skip the sunrise," I said hugging the small pillow our kids gave me for Mother's Day. "A house is a house, but Mom makes it a home," it declared in brown and red embroidered lettering. I'd been sleeping with small pillows since my big sister Deb gave me hers when she escaped home for college.

"You never skip a beach sunrise on New Year's Day," Jim said, shaking the bed as he rose.

I absently grunted agreement as my mind drifted to an easier time – the first sunrise after we bought the beach condo. That year we'd held hands watching the dawn break on our shiny-new-beach-owner lives. *Then* he'd said, "We can make it through anything as long as we keep holding hands."

I can't remember the last time we held hands.

"You better get crakalackin'. We only have twenty minutes to get Wawa coffee before the show begins." Wawa is the beloved convenience store that jump starts my days.

My feet hit the floor with a thud. "I'll wake the kids."

We bumped into each other at the end of the bed. His six-foot-four frame loomed over mine. He waved his hands impatiently for me to cross. I scurried past and out to the family room window. The sky was filled with dark grey clouds iced sparingly with silver. No color. I hoped the sunrise would be good enough – so no one would complain.

Looking right, I could see a light blue water tower with the words STONE HARBOR on it. To the left the 96th Street bridge and the bay. Forty-six minutes north was Atlantic City, where my mother grew up and later married my WWII soldier father. They were together forty-three years until he passed decades ago. She was still full of life, but not in mine.

Our beach condo view comforted and bored me. Could a person tire of their dream? I'd always wanted a Jersey beach home. But three-hour bumper-to-bumper commutes, lack of anything new to do, and day drunks by the pool had soured its splendor.

The master toilet flushed.

Or was it the person *sharing* the dream? I darted down the hall toward the smell of powdery perfume – Sienna's bedroom. She'd left *The Office* playing overnight on her flat screen. She thought the show hilarious. I'd never gotten through an episode. Its awkward depiction of work-life felt too accurate. Too familiar.

I turned off the TV and sat on her queen-sized bunk bed, which took over the room. The form under the covers moved.

"Do you still want to see the sunrise?"

She turned over and mumbled, "Yes, Mama."

I kissed her blonde bedhead. Her large brown eyes opened, and her mouth curved into a wide post-braces smile. I grinned back at my seventeen-year-old replica and said as I left, "We're leaving in ten minutes."

I opened the door to twelve-year-old Sylvie's room and sat on the bottom twin bunk. At my feet was a large paperback book titled *Arduino Robotics*. I could barely pronounce *Arduino*.

"Good morning, Lovie," No movement. "Sylvie?" A figure jolted up, eyes closed. Her short brown hair and bangs made her look a little like Harry Potter, only prettier. I put a hand on her shoulder and kissed her cheek. She smelled of last night's cheeseburger and fries – her favorite meal.

"We need to leave in five minutes if we're going to make the sunrise." I picked up her black-framed glasses from the floor and put them on the bedside table.

"Okay," she replied, falling back into bed.

I walked out to find Jim wearing a heavy wool blue pea coat, knit hat, and un-scuffed black and white sneakers. He walked past the long tan corduroy sectional toward the front door. I had to admit, with that getup and the beard, he was still a handsome specimen.

When had I stopped caring? It didn't happen at once, but slowly, like drips from a faucet. Years of misconnection had rusted and tightened it, so now nothing flowed. Even the sex had dried up. Not that I wanted *it*, but when exactly had he stopped asking?

"I'm going to warm up the Durango," Jim said, walking outside.

"We'll be right there." Back in our bedroom I put on a dumpy blue floral coat, sweats, worn tan Uggs, mittens, and a pink knit hat to hide my roots. I looked in the mirrored closet doors. No wonder he didn't want *it*. I was the heaviest I'd been in years.

*

At 7:05 a.m. we pulled out of the mostly empty condo parking lot and turned the corner to Wawa. Jim had souped up the SUV so it sounded like a helicopter taking off. He didn't care what anyone thought, including me. He just wanted it to sound *cooooool*.

He parked in front of the convenience store. I asked, "Anyone want anything?" I looked back to see Sylvie asleep and Sienna's questioning face.

"Do we have time for lattes?" she asked.

I looked at the sky. The clouds were engulfed in orange and pink tones. "Not now, but we'll get some on the way back."

"Okay," Sienna said with obvious disappointment.

"Don't worry sweet angel, we will get you a latte as soon as Mommy gets her sunrise fix," Jim said. Then to me, "Get me black coffee."

I wanted to ask for a "please" but nodded instead.

Returning a few minutes later, I put two Wawa cups in the center console. One smelled like caffeine petrol. The other, French vanilla cream.

Jim pulled the car out before I buckled and drove the three blocks to the beach parking lot. Once there, he drove toward the right side of the lifeguard shack and up the ramp toward the beach.

"You don't have the beach driving permit anymore, do you?" I whispered.

"Nah, but no one's checking today."

I felt my chest tense in an all-too-familiar way. "It isn't right to break the rules," I said loud enough for the kids to hear.

"Rules were made to be broken."

We used to agree on that.

He parked and got out. Sylvie followed.

"It's starting," Sienna said pointing toward a round yellow glow at the far edge of the clouds. I pulled my phone from a pocket. "If you're gonna post anything, make sure to get my okay first," she instructed.

I nodded agreement to our much-discussed picture-taking protocol and carefully stepped from the SUV into the sand. Pulling my hat down because of the strong Eastern breeze, I motioned for the kids to stand in front of the sun, then took a picture. Ugh. The kids' faces were in shadow because I was facing the light.

I was about to take another shot when Jim wrapped an arm around my waist. He pulled the kids in too. It should have been a perfect moment, but it felt awkward. Like we were trying too hard.

Looking at the brightening colors, I silently prayed this year would be different – better.

Within seconds Jim broke away. "It's colder than a witch's tit out here." The kids giggled. Once I laughed along too.

"Don't say things like that in front of the children," I whispered.

"Aw, you worry too much. Let's get going."

"Yeah, Mom, we're just having fun," Sylvie said, following Jim into the SUV.

Sienna put her arm around my shoulders. I leaned in and noticed her chin hovered near my nose now. Only minutes ago she'd been a high school freshman. How would I survive her departure for college in the fall?

She broke our embrace first, as always, and said, "It's cold, Mom. We better get in the car." Her eyes caught mine. "Mom, are you crying?"

"No, the wind blew sand in my eye."

"That makes sense. You never cry."

I looked back at the sunrise, wiped my cheek with a mitten, and climbed into the passenger seat.

# PART ONE

## Avidya

"Let's face it: we are excellent at self-sabotage."
*Yoga for the Creative Soul* by Erin Byron

*Chapter One*

# SHARING CIRCLES

If the Pittsburgh Steelers had been in the Super Bowl that year, I probably wouldn't have gotten divorced. Instead, my husband and I would have hosted a black-and-gold-themed party for twenty or so friends. Some would have driven Porsches (like Jim's), others hybrids or Mini Coopers (like mine). Some would have worn Steelers' gear to support our beloved team. And a few would have arrived in Philadelphia Eagles' jerseys–because the locals never won a Super Bowl.

Instead, on that early February morning, I loaded a yoga mat and overnight bag (containing an expensive screw-top red wine Jim bought by the case) into my new friend Peggy's trunk. We were going to a yoga retreat in the Berkshires. The getaway was a much-needed recharge before starting a new job the following week. It also filled my therapist's prescription to find a community of friends with similar interests – one that didn't include work, wine, or shopping. Since I spent most days (and nights) working as a corporate salesperson, the idea seemed unimaginable. A dream.

I've been in therapy since I was diagnosed with anxiety and an "all things medical" phobia in college. At times I think I don't need real friends because I pay my therapist Michelle to be one.

Looking over at Peggy, I noticed she looked younger than me even though she was a few years older. Maybe it was the purple streak in her dark pixie hair, or the Sanskrit words tattooed on her slender wrists. I met her through Jim – she was the wife of one of his Porsche car club buddies. Which may be why he was okay with me going away on a girl's weekend. He usually objected to them because I traveled so much for work. Although he didn't mind the resulting paychecks.

"Wait here a minute while I take the pups out," Peggy said as she ran into her house. She came out with two older greyhounds in tow. I nuzzled one behind the ears and the other under the chin.

"How hard is it to adopt a greyhound?" I asked, watching Peggy scoop up one dog's smelly deposit into a pink biodegradable bag.

"It's pretty difficult. You have to fill out an application and get personal references. But I know a lot of the people in the rescue group here. I could help you out."

"That would be great. Let me get back to you." I'd been wanting a dog for a while but didn't think Jim would go for it.

Peggy went into the house again and returned with Anita, a tall thin brunette with red highlights. She looked to be a size four and wore an adorable grey Lululemon outfit and designer sunglasses. I was wearing twenty-dollar XL leggings and a torn Sara Bareilles concert t-shirt.

My tendency to pull back, make fun of, and resist all things new kicked in. Was everybody at the Kripalu Yoga Institute going to be thinner and hipper than me?

Anita's once-over glance gave me the answer.

\*

Peggy and Anita spent the first few hours of the trip catching up on their kids and analyzing Anita's latest relationship. How awful it must be in the dating world. So glad I didn't have to put myself out *there*.

After a break in conversation, Anita looked down at me through the rearview mirror and asked, "So how long have you been into yoga, Donna?"

"A while." I explained my trajectory from guided meditation and yoga on DVDs to classes at the YMCA. What I didn't mention was how regular yoga practice soothed my anxiety. That despite all my body insecurity and clumsiness, at the end of every class I felt better. And yoga filled a spiritual hole left by my preacher father's fatal heart attack thirty years ago.

I sorely missed him. His quiet strength and kindness. His focus on doing the right thing, not taking the easy way out. His beautiful handwriting, deep voice, and strong silence. His belief that everyone was extraordinary – and love didn't need to be earned.

"Peggy mentioned something about you changing jobs?" Anita said.

"Yeah, I'm taking a sales job at a financial research company."

"Good for you. It's tough to find a job in finance these days. Ray is thinking of getting out of the industry altogether," Peggy said.

I got that. The finance industry has gone through many bumps in the last decade, but I was grateful to work in such a lucrative field. In undergrad, I was a theater major but by senior year realized I couldn't make a living at it. So I got my MBA. And turns out theater skills are helpful when making connections and orchestrating successful client meetings and events – the primary role of a financial salesperson. Over time, I gained a reputation for handling all types of clients, especially the difficult ones. A skill learned in childhood.

But all of that was too much to share. "I've always had an hour-long commute with lots of travel. The new company is only ten minutes from my house in West Chester, and they gave me a local territory."

The discussion moved to Sienna's departure for college. After years of effort, we'd cemented a strong relationship. We did everything together – from watching Bravo, to working out, to shopping.

After Sienna left, I would still have Sylvie at home. But I'm embarrassed to say we weren't as close. Largely because she's smarter than me.

When the kids were little, we bought the game Mouse Trap. Sienna and I struggled to put its maze-like game board together. Once constructed, we played the game with four-year-old Sylvie, but soon lost interest. We disassembled the game and put it on a bookshelf in the family room. When I came home from work the next day the Mouse Trap structure was reassembled. I asked the babysitter what had happened, and she said Sylvie had put it together by herself. Since then, she's been obsessed with building things, which eventually led to programming computers and playing complicated games constructing cities or worlds. I've tried to play with her but don't have the ability. And neither does Jim or Sienna. This left Sylvie alone a lot in front of a screen learning new computer languages or playing games with her friends. Maybe Sienna going would force us to find things in common. I hoped so. I really wanted that.

Peggy and Anita were empty-nesters, so they sympathized with my losing Sienna. Then Peggy mentioned a Reiki and crystal yoga class she went to and Anita asked where it was. I rolled my eyes when they started talking about "feeling energy." My resistance kicked in – that was too "woo woo" for me (even though I lived and died by my horoscope).

I turned toward the window and watched the barren trees fly past the highway.

*

The only evidence of the retreat center was a small road sign with the word "Kripalu" in glowing letters. We turned the car up the windy driveway and found a large, concrete, dorm-like building perched on a steep hill. Its enormous front windows overlooked a serene lake and a sign out front pointed to a nearby meditation labyrinth. Before I could ask, Peggy said it had once been a monastery.

We parked and walked toward the registration desk. I handed the young dreadlocked clerk my credit card and he gave me a form to sign promising not to wear perfume. My mouth twitched. Did lavender-vanilla body lotion count?

Keys in hand, we grabbed the bags and headed toward our rooms. Anita and Peggy were staying together. Since I didn't know them well, I'd reserved a private room.

We took the elevator to the fourth floor and separated. My room was as small as a cruise ship stateroom. I sat on the twin cot, ran my fingers over the prickly sheets, and looked around. No TV. I felt sweat form under my arms. Looking in my overnight bag for a distraction, I took out a chick-lit novel, a tattered book of poetry, two magazines, and the bottle of wine. I was about to open it when

I heard the ping of a text. Peggy. Dinner service ended in twenty minutes. I snatched my room key and ran down three flights of stairs to the cafeteria.

*

There are two food lines at Kripalu: kale and extra crunchy kale. Okay, the actual names are Non-Vegetarian and Vegetarian/Vegan. But calling what the Non-Vegetarian line offered "meat" was misleading. Only one dish on the entire twenty-foot serving line resembled chicken. The rest was a variety of vegetables, starches, and other unfamiliar items. And there was kale. Lots of kale.

I hate kale.

During dinner I chewed on my food (which was surprisingly yummy) and the decision to come to this place. It was way out of my comfort zone. Kripalu's website advertised a tranquil spa-like atmosphere, but the concrete block walls, perfume restrictions, and scratchy sheets made me feel like I'd fallen into a Buddhist boot camp.

And I *really* hate camping.

*

The next morning, I headed downstairs to the cafeteria for coffee before the 6:30 yoga class. Nothing. I headed to the reception desk hoping to get a cup of employee coffee before regular coffee service started. I asked the curly-grey-haired woman with wire-rimmed glasses if that was possible. She peered over her spectacles. After a moment of awkward silence, she said that to support those detoxing from caffeine they only provided coffee in the café – which opened at 8:00 a.m. Even though my mind was screaming un-yoga-like thoughts, I nodded silently and slumped away.

After stumbling upstairs to the intermediate yoga class, I kicked off my shoes at the cubbies and paused to read the black and white sign by the door. The class lasted ninety minutes. I was used to hour sessions. How would I go that long un-caffeinated?

As we began, the slim ponytailed instructor asked us how we felt. It seemed like a strange question. No instructor had asked me that before. Why does it matter how I feel?

She prompted us to "find our edge" between what we could and couldn't do. When we got to that edge, we were to soften and surrender into the pose for as long as we could.

After about the twentieth downward dog, my arms were shaking. I was about to *surrender* to the café – and the sweet bliss of caffeine – when the instructor came over. She rubbed her hands together and placed them on my wrists. Her touch felt awkward, but soon the pain subsided. Before I could say thank you, she pulled away and returned to the front of the class.

When she cued us to stand in mountain pose, my gaze drifted outside. The sun was rising. Large feathery flakes fell through tree-branch veins. It was mesmerizing. Had snow always looked like this? Or had I never stopped to notice?

The chattering in my head slowed. I came here confident I knew what yoga was, but this was something different. Not just postures and breathing, but an in-and-out-of-body experience.

Moments later the teacher cued the end of class and suggested we get comfy on the floor with bolsters and blankets. I was both exhausted and peaceful. And hungry.

I met Peggy and Anita by the shoe cubbies and walked with them to the cafeteria. When I mentioned the instructor touching my hands, Peggy said, "That was Reiki. She was giving you the energy to go on."

Maybe Reiki wasn't so "woo woo" after all. I made a mental note to read more about it.

We enjoyed a tasty kale-free breakfast heavy on vegan baked goods and long on silence. Kripalu urged guests to refrain from talking during meals to allow for mindful eating. On the way out of the cafeteria, Sienna texted me from home. I broke off from my friends to call her.

When I returned to the cafeteria, Peggy and Anita were gone. Alone, I looked at the seminar schedule and found a "must-attend" session called Kripalu Sharing Circle. I made my way down to the basement and entered a windowless room with grey tiles and a musty smell.

About ten people were sitting on the floor in a circle. Each one was leaning on a black cushion with a stiff chair-like back. The moderator, who had a grey pageboy and thick black glasses, shut the door and sat facing the group. The session, she said, was an opportunity to share something briefly. Once each person finished, the rest of the circle members were not to respond. We were only to provide a safe space. What's said in the sharing circle stayed in the sharing circle. My gaze wandered down to the grey tiles. What could I share?

***

My first clear memory of Mother is from the Sunday after my big sister Deb left for college. I was four and Deb was fourteen years older than me. I used to think she was my Mama because she took care of me all the time. But she was just my sister. That's why it was okay for her to leave me.

I see Daddy. He's standing at the pulpit wearing a black robe with a purple satin-looking scarf. He looks at me and smiles. I throw him a kiss. I'm so proud of my Daddy.

His head bows and he reads from the big Bible I'm not allowed to touch. Mother is beside me. She is wearing a blue-flowered dress because she loves flowers. I'm wearing a stiff skirt with a white sweater. I'm so excited because I've never spent so much time with Mother or been allowed in adult church before. Up until now, I've always stayed in the nursery during services.

Daddy talks about how Jesus felt dying on the cross. His words make me squirm. I start kicking the top of my buckled shoe on the pew in front of us. Mother grabs my hand and squeezes it hard. "Stay still," she says. How can she talk with her teeth together like that?

I pull my hand away and dive underneath the pew toward Daddy. I always play under the benches when Daddy practices his sermons on Saturdays; I crawl to the front of the church and he laughs and picks me up and hugs me.

Not today. Mother grabs my ankles and drags me back toward her. The course rug scrapes my knees and I cry out. By the time she settles me back in the pew, I'm rubbing my brush-burned knees and weeping softly.

"Stop it," she says. I look into her scary steel-blue eyes and cry louder.

She drags me from the pew and down the aisle of the church. Some churchgoers stare as we pass. Others look away.

Down the stairs to the first floor we fly. Past the Sunday school rooms with tan partitions and grey tiled floors. Down the middle stairs to the musty basement bathroom no one uses – two floors below the sanctuary and far from the first-floor nursery in the back of the building. Down where no one can hear.

Mother opens the door of one of the old wooden stalls and pulls me inside. She drops the toilet seat and sits, then throws me on her lap, bottom side up. The rusty screws that hold the white porcelain toilet to the floor are close to my face. I'm afraid of rust – Mother told me it causes tetanus, and you can die from that.

I try to tell her, but her hand is already in motion. The force of the strike makes my eyes water and my stomach roil. I try to scramble off her lap, but she anchors me with her right arm and continues.

I cry for help, but no one comes.

*** 

The room grew tense as the sharing circle participants told their stories. It felt awkward to hear them and not provide comfort. One recently divorced woman was struggling to make a living running a yoga studio. She'd come to Kripalu to learn techniques to help her business. It was hard for me to relate. *Why couldn't she just keep her marriage together?*

After she spoke, the leader told everyone to breathe in what she'd said. Breathing in her feelings and exhaling comfort settled me. The next speaker recently lost her husband to cancer. As the stories streamed, the space warmed. To my surprise, I felt like sharing too. But the thought made my cheeks burn.

When the silence between stories lengthened, I took a deep breath and said something only my family and Michelle knew. "I come from a long line of abuse." My voice stalled for a moment and then came back. "My mother was removed from her mother's house as a child because she was abused. Then she physically and verbally abused me."

I looked at the shocked faces and decided not to add that

her paternal grandparents raised her. Because after her parents separated, her father died - from excessive alcohol use.

The room was quiet. No one interrupted or told their own tale. They just gave me space to tell mine. My throat relaxed. "But this story has a happy ending." I shared that Sienna called earlier because a friend had hurt her. And after we talked it through, she decided not to retaliate. Instead, she was taking time to figure out how to communicate her feelings without losing the friendship.

Even a decade ago, I would have wrecked a relationship if something similar happened to me. And Mother? I don't remember *her* having friends.

"I'm so proud of her. We're breaking the pattern." The eyes looking at me were kind, supportive. I was surprised. I had never been heard like that outside of therapy. "Uh… thank you for listening."

As the next person spoke, I hugged my knees to my chest. Why had I shared that? Could it be this place – or was it the yoga?

Whenever I saw someone from the circle during the rest of the retreat, they nodded but didn't say anything.

It was like it never happened. But I felt different, freer.

Because my secret was out.

*

Later that day, I attended a seminar titled "No Excuses" based on the book by Brian Tracy. The description said, "Most people think success comes from good luck or enormous talent, but many successful people achieve their accomplishments in a simpler way: through self-discipline. *No Excuses!* shows how to achieve success in all three major areas of life, including personal, business and money goals, as well as overall happiness." Sounded perfect.

I entered the presentation room and sat on one of the cushioned metal chairs. Anita was a few chairs away. I gave her a small wave.

The moderator told us to think about things we wished to do but lacked the time, money, or motivation. He asked us to write something we wanted more than anything else – something we would do with "no excuses." What would I do? More to the point, what would I do if I didn't have to answer to Jim? The answer surprised me.

The moderator asked us to share our "no excuses" item with someone else. Feeling more comfortable with someone I knew, I gravitated toward Anita. I was nervous, so I asked her to share first.

When it was my turn, I felt a little breathless. "I want to become a yoga teacher." Since my dad died, I'd found it hard to go back to church because it reminded me of him. But something about this simple, reverent place was familiar – comforting. Maybe digging into something like yoga training would fill the spiritual hole in my life.

And more importantly, it would give me something to do when Sienna left.

But Anita's expression stopped me from sharing any of that. "Really?" She started to say something else but stopped. "Oh great," she smiled. "You go for it."

I thanked her but immediately felt a stiffness in my neck. Did she have the same doubts I did? How would I fit teacher training into my busy work life? And how would I become graceful or body-confident enough to pose in front of a class?

And finally, what was Jim going to say?

*Chapter Two*

# MEATLOAF

The next day the tires on my Mini Cooper swerved as I entered the icy driveway. I parked in the garage and looked over at the 1968 Mustang convertible Jim gifted me for our twentieth anniversary. I had no idea why. I never asked for it.

When Jim and I met, my dad had just died, and I was broke. Soon after, my career took off and Jim grew a successful company of his own. Over the years we'd gradually spent larger and larger amounts of money on jewelry, designer clothes, home remodels, and eventually a beach condo. But a few years ago, I traded in my seven-series BMW for a Mini Cooper. The cost of maintaining the luxury car was ridiculous, and a vehicle with a higher mpg was better for the environment.

Now the price of *all* our material things seemed too high. Maybe I'd run out of things to desire or was seeking something else, but the austere Kripalu experience had changed me. It opened my soul in a way I couldn't yet describe.

Maybe another way of life was possible, even desirable.

I took a long inhale – and exhale. I didn't want to go in, but after a few minutes realized no one was coming out (or cared). After gathering my bags from the trunk, I walked into the kitchen. Jim was sitting on a leather bar stool swirling red wine in a large glass. He was wearing a silky t-shirt with a designer zipped hoodie and jeans. And a Porsche baseball cap. *Top Gear*, a British race car show, was on the flat-screen TV. Jim was an amateur Porsche race car driver, or as he liked to say, "I like to drive real fast in circles with my friends."

I sat my bags down and kissed him on the cheek, hoping he was in a good mood.

He put an arm around my waist without looking away from the TV. A tall pot-bellied balding man on the screen was revealing drive times on a long scoreboard. I waited for Jim to say something, but the show entranced him.

"Hey, would you mind watching that upstairs so I can catch up on Bravo while making dinner?" Why hadn't he asked about my weekend or, come to think of it, tried to call me while I was away?

He silently handed over the remote and took my bags upstairs. I watched him withdraw.

As I sat sipping his wine, I tried to recall what Kripalu felt like.

*

I hate meatloaf. Chopping up all those vegetables and forming that sticky mess into a loaf. But it was Jim's favorite. And I did the cooking.

He ate every bite as always, but didn't say thank you or comment on the taste. Instead, he detailed the litany of things he'd done around the house while I was gone and pointed out the baskets of laundry to be folded.

I decided there was no good time to start the conversation.

Jumping in feet first was the best course. "I want to become a yoga teacher."

He looked over at Sienna and said, "Oh, here's another of your mother's projects." She and Sylvie laughed, then saw my dark expression and went back to eating. Sylvie poured more ketchup on her last piece of meatloaf.

I picked up the salt and pepper shakers and put them on the stove. "And after yoga teacher training, I might train to become a yoga therapist. I just read an article about a yoga therapy center for cancer."

"Now Donna, who's gonna pay you for yogurt therapy?"

I hated when he said that. Yogurt.

I picked up two plates slick with ketchup and hamburger grease and dropped them into the sink. I flipped the faucet and watched the water make a hole in the debris. "Who's going to pay you to drive a race car?" I snapped. "But I'm supportive of that."

"Well, you can do it as long as it doesn't take you away from the kids too much."

I grudgingly said thank you. Where was his fatherly concern the two weekends a month he was off racing and partying with his buddies? Was he afraid yoga might cut into his fun?

Of course, I didn't ask. That would cause a fight. Instead I turned off the water and walked away.

\*

Over the next couple weeks, I searched the internet for a yoga training program that fit into my work and home schedule. All the programs took up to two hundred and fifty hours and cost anywhere from two to three thousand dollars. Most required one three-day weekend of classes per month, which I knew Jim wouldn't go for. Then I remembered my favorite YMCA yoga teacher, Mary, talking about her twelve-month program, which required one afternoon training session and two short workshops per month. It also gave students unlimited access to yoga classes. I called Mary and she recommended I meet with the school leader.

I mentioned the program to Jim, and he grunted. I took that as a yes and scheduled a meeting with the head of the school.

*

My heart beat loudly as I turned the car into the yoga school driveway. The parking lot was lined with flowering pear and cherry trees. Walking up to the second floor of the building, I entered the lobby and felt embraced by shelves and shelves of books. The space reminded me of my father's study, where I used to read while he prepared his sermons. And where we both hid from Mother.

A ponytailed, tie-dye-wearing receptionist looked up from behind a cluttered wooden desk. I asked for Yoga Rob. Minutes later, a tall, athletic man with curly grey hair greeted me. His smile reminded me of a laughing Buddha.

After settling us cross-legged in one of the yoga rooms, Yoga Rob asked what brought me in. Why I wanted to teach yoga. I told him how yoga practice soothed my anxiety and how I wanted to help others manage theirs. And that my father had been a minister — and this was a way to bring spirituality back into my life. I *didn't* share that I hoped yoga training would give me something to do when Sienna left for college. That felt too needy.

Yoga Rob shared multiple success stories of middle-aged female yogi transformation – and an hour later – I left heavier with an eight-inch stack of yoga books and lighter by two-and-a-half grand.

*

By my next visit a month later, the spring blooms had given way to waxy green leaves. In the packed parking lot, I parked between a sage green Prius and an indigo blue Subaru. They sported "Kindness matters" and "Coexist" bumper stickers. My bright red Mini Cooper with its MINIDVA license plate looked like something from a Sesame Street skit. The one where they sing "One of These Things is Not Like the Other."

Inside the training room with its purple walls and large skylights, I felt self-conscious. Mostly slender women were warming up on their multi-colored yoga mats, some with small stones and feathers in the corners. They reminded me of hippie ballet dancers. My insecurities and resistance were in full force. Hopefully, I could stifle them to open to the possibilities here.

Yoga Rob sat silently, cross-legged, at the front of the classroom. The students started to notice him and grew quiet. Once the room was still, he led us in a brief breathing meditation. Then he launched us into a discussion of yoga philosophy.

"What does non-attachment mean?" he asked.

Multiple hands rose. Yoga Rob called on a lithe blonde thirty-something in the front row. "It means to do your best without worrying about the outcome," she said.

"Yes, yes. But is there more?" Yoga Rob asked.

More hands rose. I dug mine under a blanket. An older woman with long red hair and wide-legged paisley pants said, "You need to detach yourself from the outcome and let the universe take over."

The discussion reminded me of dinner when I was a kid. Except back then, we spoke of God, not the universe. "Leave your life in the hands of our holy father," Daddy would say. When I was thirteen, I preached a sermon of my own as part of a youth service. The topic was the Second Coming. I still remember the chilled silence when I described empty chairs rocking on a porch after believers had been spirited to heaven. Afterward, Daddy told my brother Carl that I would be the most spiritual of all his children. I'm sure that came as a surprise, as Carl was in seminary at the time.

Yoga Rob went from non-attachment to the idea of being in the present moment. Everything that matters is right here, right now. Looking for specific outcomes or grasping for something other than what's in front of us leads to suffering. These pronouncements didn't make sense to me. They sounded like gibberish. I didn't even bother to write them down.

During the following yoga practice, the teacher kept teasing us to work harder. To hold poses longer and push through our resistance and pain. I made sarcastic comments under my breath. Then I got hot and angry and fantasized about walking out. But was glad I didn't. Because at the end of class, as we lay in relaxation, she said something I've never forgotten - that how we are on the mat is how we are in real life. We show up for both the same way. If we want to make changes in our lives, the mat is the place to practice.

It is where transformation begins.

*

While packing my mat and props at the end of the day, I overheard a young student complaining about the required monthly essay assignments. She said she hated writing. Others agreed. I stayed silent.

I loved writing.

Since age six, I'd been writing and stopped only after Jim broke into my computer and read part of a "fictional" scene composed for an online mystery writer's workshop. I'd wanted to be the next Janet Evanovich or maybe even Lisa Scottoline.

For that class assignment I'd used one of our real-life arguments as inspiration. The privacy invasion we both felt led to a heated fight, one of many around that time. That night, alone in the guest room, I'd researched divorce lawyers on my phone but didn't call any. I wasn't ready to risk our financially carefree life and beach house. And I needed him to take care of the kids so I could travel for work.

So, we made up. I promised not to write about him. And stopped writing altogether.

Until now.

# Chapter Three

# LITTLE PINK POSTCARD

The first week of June, I had Sienna's graduation ceremony and party and a final sales presentation at a famous amusement park (which required a one-day round trip to Orlando). It felt like I was performing some working mom triathlon.

The reward for this parenting trifecta was our first trip as a family out of the country – a vacation in Bermuda. I loved traveling. Jim hated it. After I'd taken the kids to London, Rome, and Paris by myself, he was finally joining us on a trip. It gave me hope that he could change. That we could create a *happy* empty nest.

And compromise our disparate views on almost everything.

\*

Several days into the Bermuda trip, I dipped my key card into our hotel door slot over and over. It wouldn't open. I was paying four-hundred and fifty dollars a night for the room but couldn't get inside. I stomped my foot and banged on the white-paneled door. A rustling noise came from the lock, and the door opened. Sienna, who had just turned eighteen, stood in an Instagram-ready blue-and-white striped bikini with full makeup. Sylvie was sitting in khaki shorts and a pink Pokémon t-shirt on one of the two queen-sized beds, laptop computer open.

"Where's your dad?" I asked Sienna in a tight voice.

"He's on the balcony taking a business call on my phone. Why does he keep doing that?" Sienna said.

"He's trying to sell the business."

"I don't understand why he couldn't use your phone for calls while we're here. Or why he won't upgrade from a flip phone so he can get international service."

"I don't know. But Dad pays for your phone, so you gotta deal with it." I watched her face fall and lips protrude. "I'm sorry to be so short." I hugged her. She hugged me back. "Want to head down to the beach?"

"Once I get my phone back."

"Okay, okay. Let's get everything together, and then you can ask your father for the phone." I touched Sylvie's shoulder, "Lovie, do you want to go to the beach?"

She looked up from the computer. "No, Mom. I'll stay here with Dad." It was day three of our trip to Bermuda, and Sylvie had spent most of it playing Minecraft with her friends online.

I turned away and gently pulled a pink-and-yellow-flowered one-piece swimsuit and matching skirt from my mostly repacked suitcase. "This is my last night here because I have to fly to Chicago tomorrow, so we should do something together tonight. Without phones or computers."

"We could go up to the indoor pool by the spa and watch the sunset together," Sienna suggested.

"That would be nice," Jim said as he walked in from the balcony wearing a short-sleeved shirt with a shark on it and khaki shorts.

"Your mom and I watched the sunset most every night on our honeymoon."

My eyes caught his. I was surprised to feel warmth spread down my body.

"Dad, can I have my phone back?" Sienna said.

He quickly pushed a few buttons on it and handed it back to her. "Thank you, pumpkin."

"We're going to the beach. Want to come?" I asked.

"Is Sylvie coming?"

"No, she wants to stay here."

"Then I'll take a nap." He was snoring before we left the room.

*

"Come on, the pool's up here," Sienna said that evening as she ran up the stairs to the spa. "I found it yesterday."

"Oh, wow. This is beautiful," I said. The pool was indoors but it had windows on all sides with a clear view of the beach.

"Last one in's a loser," Jim said as he cannonballed into the deep end of the pool. I laughed and sat on the rim of the pool as the kids followed him.

Jim swam over and led me into the water. It was warm, and I could see blue and green tiled fish shapes on the pool bottom. I couldn't stand without slipping below the surface, so Jim put his arms around me. He kissed my lips.

"Ugh. Don't do that," Sienna said.

"We have to pick this up again when you get home from Chicago," he whispered.

"Wish I didn't have to go to the conference," I said. Surprisingly, I meant it.

"It's okay. Gotta make the moolahs." We both laughed.

"Hey Dad," Sylvie said, "the sun is setting."

"Wow. Sometimes it's good to look away from the computer."
Sylvie nodded.

Jim looked at the sunset, then down at my face, "Love you."

"Love you too."

*

Two days later, I made my way through the bustling airport security line in Chicago. Sienna's angry voice squeaked through my headphones. "Mom, Dad lost it in customs at the Bermuda airport. I was sure he was going to get arrested 'cause he wouldn't stop talking on my phone. You're not allowed to have phones out in the customs line."

"But you made it through okay, right?" I pulled out my laptop computer to put it in a bin for the scanners.

"Yeah, but they went through all our luggage. They pulled out everything, even my underwear. It was so embarrassing."

I heard a loudspeaker through the phone. "Are things okay now?"

"Yeah. We're on the plane. I would have texted sooner, but Dad kept taking my phone. Wish you were here."

"Me too," I lied. "I'm leaving Chicago soon, so we'll all be home tonight." I paused for a moment, then said, "Can you hand the phone to your father?'

I heard crackling noises as the phone was handed over. "Hey," he said. "I hate traveling. Customs was a bitch."

His voice was louder than Sienna's. I turned down the volume so the Chicago TSA officer in front of me wouldn't hear. "I know you do. Everything okay?"

"Yup. Why?"

"Sienna said you were making phone calls."

He hesitated then said, "Just trying to do some bidness. We

gotta pay for this trip. I got the hotel bill. I had no idea the place was so expensive. You shouldn't have spent that much."

"It was worth it. And who knows when Sienna will want to travel with us again."

"She'll always want to go with us – especially if we're paying."

I laughed, "You're probably right. Tell Sienna to text me when you take off and land." Jim didn't believe in texting.

"I will. Did everything go okay in Chicago?"

"Got a few follow-up meetings. Not as many as I'd like. But all good." I could hear the flight attendant announcing the cabin doors were closing. "You better go. Love you."

"Love you too."

Once safely through security, I found my favorite restaurant and ordered a margarita on the rocks, guacamole, and chips. Scrolling through the Bermuda pictures, I saw Sienna and me at the beach. A rare one of Sylvie outside building sandcastles. The family together at dinner, taken by a server. An even rarer one of me kissing Jim. Things were falling into place. Some part of me wanted to boast about our loving, stable nuclear family. I uploaded the pictures to Facebook. (Yes, they were Sienna-approved).

*

The next morning, I watched from the bed as Jim put on his gardening attire – ragged jeans, an old t-shirt, and paint-spattered sneakers. We'd just coupled in that old married way. Our dance wasn't slow, as the kids could walk in at any time, but intense enough to knock out any lingering frustrations or doubts. Jim was especially attentive to my needs – even threw in some new moves. I was tingly and content.

Jim kissed me and left. There was a thunderstorm brewing, and he wanted to get the yard work done before it hit. I never thought of offering to join him in his garden endeavors. Instead, I put on exercise clothes and sneakers and headed to the kitchen. Since both kids were asleep, I made a cup of coffee and looked at my reading pile. It included a couple mysteries, a book of Robert Frost poetry (I found reading poems soothing), and my yoga reading for the month on the Yamas — core yoga principles including non-violence, truthfulness, moderation, non-stealing, and non-greed. They reminded me of the ten commandments. Daddy always said the commandments were there to keep us out of trouble.

The Yama that stuck with me the most was Satya – which meant being impeccable with our words. Or not speaking so we don't hurt others or make things happen that we could later regret. I had never seen being silent as a choice before. Growing up, it always felt like a punishment – and Mother had never been careful with her words.

Around noon I walked out to the mailbox. I'd held the mail while in Bermuda, and the carrier had left it all in a white plastic USPS bin. As I divided it into piles on the kitchen counter, a pink postcard caught my eye. I'd seen similar ones, all from the florist Jim used. I turned it over, assuming it was a reminder for him to send flowers to his mom. It was her birthday the following month.

As I read the card, my hands started to shake. Within the paragraph of black printed text was a name, Daniella. He sent flowers last year for her birthday. This was a friendly reminder to do it again.

I had no idea who she was. But my husband was sending her flowers.

*Chapter Four*

# BAD BLOOD

I put my hand on the edge of the kitchen counter and slid down the cabinet to the floor. I crossed my legs as if in meditation. My stomach churned from the smell of intimacy. He'd learned some new *tricks*. Was she the teacher?

It might have been how I was seated, or divine intervention, but the yoga reading about Satya popped into my mind. Normally I would have screamed at him. Even threatened divorce.

Instead, I realized I needed to be careful with my words. They could change everything.

Sylvie, seated in front of the desktop in the family room, yelled at one of her gaming friends to go faster. I wanted to yell too, but flew out the door to the garage instead, pink postcard in hand. Curling the edge of it in my fingers, I looked at the '68 Mustang. Had he bought it out of guilt?

Outside I could see tree branches swaying – the storm was settling in.

I hated when couples played out family dramas on the front lawn. But the kids were inside, and I couldn't let this one slide.

The sound of the lawn mower drifted back and forth with my husband's journey. I watched as he floated in and out of my sight.

Suddenly the door slammed shut behind me. Jim heard the noise and turned off the machine.

I held my breath as he walked over. His clothes were sweaty and his unshaven face smudged with dirt. He could sometimes forget how massive he was. I never did.

"What's up?" he asked.

I held up the pink postcard. "Do you have something to tell me?"

He read the card and his forehead crinkled. A pained softness crossed his face. He sat down on an old plastic step stool with a broken handle. "Yes, I guess I do."

I stayed quiet. *Be careful with your words.*

He kept talking. The affair had been over for months. She didn't mean anything to him. He'd gotten into it when his business had been in trouble the year before, when I wasn't there for him.

*You're blaming this on me?!* I found my words. "How long was the affair?" My eyes felt wide open.

"I don't know, six months maybe."

My arms and legs trembled. They were saying "run!" but I needed to know. "How did you meet?

"On the internet."

"On a dating site?" My voice was shrill. It sounded like someone else was talking.

"Yeah. For married people." He looked at my face and then at the cement garage floor.

We'd talked about sealing the cracks, but never had.

*

I fled into the house. Thinking of comfort, I grabbed a bottle of cabernet from the wine fridge. Then walked into the orange and grey living room. It had recently been converted into a "she den." Grabbing the TV remote, I turned on *Real Housewives of New York*.

I texted my best friend, Hope, the news. In the background, several of the housewives were gossiping about one woman's cheating husband. Why did I watch these shows?

My cell phone rang. Hope. I swiped to answer.

"What happened?" Hope asked before I could say hello. I muted the TV.

"Jim's cheating on me with some woman he met on a dating site for married people."

"I didn't even know there was such a thing."

"Me neither. But it all makes sense. The nights he paid the babysitter to work late while I was traveling. Why he stopped making hotel reservations for race weekends on my Hilton Honors account. The incessant calls on Sienna's phone while we were in Bermuda. The way he kept buying me expensive presents." Like the Mustang. "Then there was that anonymous email I got last year from someone saying he was cheating on me."

"You got an email?"

"Yeah. I showed it to him, but he denied anything was going on. Said it was spam. And I believed him. I'm so stupid." I looked up to see the RHONY women on one of their luxury beach vacations. I need a vacation from my life.

"You're not stupid. You just didn't want it to be true."

She was right. I didn't want to believe it. Or for the kids to suffer. "We were getting along so well in Bermuda. I thought we were going to be okay." The TV screen started to blur.

"What are you going to do? Are you going to stay with him?"

"I don't know." Then I remembered. "Oh, my God, I just posted all those pictures of us on Facebook. How embarrassing."

"You shouldn't be embarrassed. *You've* done nothing wrong."

"Not yet, but I could. I want to kill him right now." How would that look on my yoga teacher resume?

She paused. Then said, "Maybe you should go to the shore house. Get some space between you. See how you feel."

*

At the door of our bedroom, I paused. The sheets were rumpled, his pajamas still on the floor. The sight forced me from the room. I stomped down the hall to Sienna's bedroom.

She was lying awake in bed. When she saw my face, she sat up, "Mom what's wrong?"

I shook my head and sat next to her. I started to cry.

"What happened?" She pulled me into her arms and patted my back – the way I usually did for her.

Divorce "experts" tell you not to act out of anger, fear, or sorrow. Why? Because emotional decisions are the ones you'll regret – long after the last decree is signed.

But I didn't know that yet.

"Your father cheated on me with some woman he met on the internet."

"What!?" I nodded and fell back in her arms. "I'm so sorry, Mom. What're you going to do?"

"I don't know. But I can't stay here now." *I'm afraid of what I will do to your father.* "Hope says I should go to the beach."

She jumped out of bed. "Well, let's go. Girls trip!" My chest eased a little. I had hoped she'd come too.

I gave her a long hug. Then we separated to pack.

On the way out the door I kissed Sylvie on the head. She pulled her earphones off and asked, "Where you going?"

"To the beach," Sienna said.

"Do I have to come?" she asked.

"No, you can stay here with your father."

"Good." She turned back to her computer and said, "Love you." She put her headphones back on.

I wrapped my arms around her shoulders from behind. Her warmth and the lingering smell of peanut butter and waffles comforted me. "Love you too." I headed out to the garage and started loading the car.

The smell of fresh-cut grass made me hesitate. I couldn't believe it. How could he continue cutting the grass after our conversation?

"Where you going?" Jim asked walking in from the driveway.

"To the beach house." Before he could respond, Sienna walked into the garage with her overnight bag. She looked at her father. Then turned her back and threw her bag in the car. A smile crept over my face as I watched Jim's body wilt. Before getting in the driver's seat, I yelled back to him, "Better get out of the way."

I put the car in reverse and drove off.

\*

Driving to the shore, I kept changing Sirius channels. All the songs made me weepy. My iTunes playlists weren't any better. Pink's "True Love." "Crazy Lucky" by Better Than Ezra. I didn't feel lucky in love anymore. More like crazy angry. Jim calls me "the Kraken" when I get like this, after the creature in *Pirates of the Caribbean*. After about twenty channel switches Sienna plugged her phone into the USB port and selected a Taylor Swift album. We sang the chorus of "Bad Blood" together.

Traffic was heavy, so we arrived at the shore condo around dinnertime. I immediately went into Jim's closet and pulled down one of his precious two-hundred-dollar wines from the top shelf. As I searched for a corkscrew, I noticed his expensive expresso machine. He loved that thing. Next to it was a cinnamon grater he'd ordered from some shishi gourmet site. I seized them both and erupted from the front door of the condo. Within seconds I'd slammed the grater and cappuccino pot into the garbage chute down the hall. Then the expresso machine. It banged and clanged as it fell into the bin. I giggled thinking how pissed Jim would be when he realized it was gone.

Sienna was at the condo entrance when I returned. She didn't say anything as I brushed past.

I struggled with the wine, managing to pull out half the dried-up cork. Then took a steak knife to push the rest in. I found a decanter, poured in the wine, and raised it to my lips.

Out of the corner of my eye I saw my soon-to-be-college-co-ed watching. I slowly put the decanter down. I smiled to reassure her and took a wine glass from the cupboard. After filling it to the brim, I lowered myself into the chaise portion of the sectional that easily sat four. It would fit three even better.

On my second glass of wine, I asked Sienna to hit the Wawa around the corner for some cheese curls. By the time she got back I was pouring my third glass.

I don't remember anything else.

*Chapter Five*

# FIRE PIT

Early the next morning I woke to the crash of beer bottles falling into a garbage truck. Fred's Tavern across the street. I tried to open my eyes but the blinding light from the unshaded window held me back. Or maybe it was my blistering headache and Triscuit tongue. I struggled across the black and white tiled floor to the sink to get water. Then looked down at the cheese curl crumbs and red wine drops on the metal sink. Like a tornado, everything from the previous day descended.

My phone said it was Sunday at 8 a.m. Normally I'd be exercising on the elliptical machine in our basement. Instead, I walked down the hall and opened Sienna's bedroom door. Light snores greeted me. When had she gone to bed? What had happened before? When would I learn wine doesn't solve anything?

I walked back through the family room to the balcony and opened the door. It was chilly for June. Could I get in a walk before we go home?

I sat down on one of the brown rattan patio chairs. Would I have to give up beach walks and the condo because of Jim's cheating?

And was I mad about the adultery, or that we hadn't divorced years ago? I put my hands on my face. The hollows beneath my eyes felt hard and uncomfortable. I snatched my phone and dialed him.

"When are you coming home?" he asked.

"Tonight, but you have to leave." My voice trembled. "I can't look at you, and it's not fair *I* can't be in the house. *You* cheated, not me."

"Okay, okay. But where am I going to go?"

"I don't give a shit."

*

When we got home four hours later, the driveway was empty. Sylvie was in the same spot as when we left. In the family room by the computer. Sienna and I dragged our suitcases into the kitchen. When Sylvie didn't notice, I said loudly, "Hey Lovie, we're home."

She put her headphones down and came over to hug me. "Mom, why'd you leave yesterday? And do you know why Dad left with his suitcase?"

Sienna pulled her into her arms. They hugged so long Sylvie looked up at me. "You have to tell her," Sienna said.

I shook my head no. She was too young.

"Do you want me to say it?"

I hesitated. It was going to come out anyway. "Your father cheated on me."

"Like in a game?"

"No, you idiot, like in a marriage. Dad had an affair with someone else."

"Sienna, don't call your sister an idiot."

Sylvie looked at me. "Are you okay?"

"Yeah. I'm okay. We're all okay. But I need your Dad out of the house for a little while."

"Okay." She started to shift back and forth on her feet, then turned back to the computer. "What are we havin' for dinner?" She sat down in front of the screen. Sylvie is oblivious to facial expressions, so she doesn't react much to conflict. I think that might be her superpower.

I looked at Sienna. "Whatever emoji," she said, shrugging her shoulders. I watched as she dragged her suitcase upstairs.

"Sylvie, we'll order pizza for us and a cheeseburger for you."

She put her headphones back on. "And fries. They always forget the fries."

*

I hauled my suitcase upstairs to the master bedroom and noticed Jim's crystal driving award on the dresser. It was about eight inches long and shaped like a teardrop. I shifted it between my hands. How many times had he taken his mistress on those weekend racing trips? *I wonder if I could get away with bludgeoning him like those scorned spouses on murder mystery shows?*

Afraid I might act on that impulse, I hurried down the hall and hid the award in an office filing cabinet. When I got back to the bedroom, I saw an email from Jim on my phone. He wanted to come home.

"Fuck that!" I started walking through the house pulling framed pictures of us off the bookshelves and piano. In the entryway I spotted our wedding vow renewal pictures, mounted on wooden block frames for all to see. I ripped them down and gathered all the images on a couch in the basement. Steps away from the fire pit outside.

I put a fire starter in the pit, surrounded it with newspaper, and lit a match. Once the fire was raging, I went to get the pictures.

First, I undid the frame latches and threw the smaller ones in.

Next the larger renewal ceremony pictures. When I got to my favorite one, I carefully lowered it on top of the blaze. It showed low-carb-diet-skinny me with a short pixie cut wearing a rack sale Vera Wang wedding dress. That was the last time I was that thin, or my hair that short. I'd consumed a lot of wine and carbs since then. What else had I been stuffing down? Maybe the urge to divorce him?

Flames danced around the picture. Suddenly a billow of smoke burst through my heart and orange, yellow, and greenish-blue flames melted the frame.

"That was awesome," Sienna said. I hadn't noticed her sitting on the brick wall around the fire pit.

"Mom, when is the food coming?" Sylvie yelled from the deck door.

"Is that all she cares about?" Sienna asked.

"At least that will never change."

*

Monday morning, I snuck into my office and quietly closed the door to avoid chit-chat. I didn't care about the weather. And damn sure didn't want to talk about my weekend.

Looking toward the desk, I noticed a framed picture of the kids. It was from an Outer Banks summer vacation a decade or so before. Jim and I had fought the whole time. I'd considered leaving him then too. Could I do it now? Or would I back out? Again.

Why was I hesitating? Was it fear that I couldn't stand on my own? Or because deep down, under all the anger, was a crusty layer of sad. Sad because he'd betrayed us and we're no longer a team. Sad because I couldn't ask him what to do next. Sad because he alone knew how to drag me out of a funk – by tap-dancing on the furniture or going round the corner to get Reese's. And hurt. He'd been focusing those talents on someone else.

Finally – and maybe most importantly – I was miserable because we'd gone so far off course. After twenty-two years, and diligent parenting of two adorable munchkins, we'd come to a place where it felt wrong to wear his ring.

I looked down at my left hand. In place of the wedding band that had "Dreams Come True" inscribed in cursive around the inside was a blue enamel circle, I'd bought in Rome. If anyone asked, I'd say our band was being resized – like my life.

Logging into the computer, I immediately cringed. A bar chart of my year-to-date sales numbers was on the home page next to all the other sales reps'. I wasn't last - but far from first. It was going to take time to build the relationships to close that gap. We'd put aside money to withstand a slow first year of sales. But that was with the expectation that Jim would carry the weight of the expenses. What would happen if we got a divorce?

I started Googling divorce and found a list of recommended books: *Divorce: Think Financially, Not Emotionally; A Complete Guide to Fast Divorce;* and *Getting Past Your Breakup.*

I added *How to Survive the Loss of a Love* to the list. A friend had given it to me decades earlier after my grandfather died. It taught me so many things, including the five stages of grief and the benefits of a good hot bath. I'd gifted my last copy to a friend, and needed another.

After buying the books online, I ordered CDs of Billy Joel's greatest hits. I needed music that didn't remind me of Jim, and most of Joel's hits were released before we met.

Now what? I walked over to the door, opened it, and rubbed my back against the frame. My skin was itchy and peeling from

Bermuda sunburn. After my dad died, Mother said one of the hardest things was when her back was itchy. No one was there to scratch it. It seemed silly at the time.

Now I understood.

*

It was after six when I got home. Jim's blue Durango was in the driveway - erasing any end-of-the-workday jubilation. As soon as I pulled my Mini Cooper into the garage, Sienna came out to greet me.

"Dad's home," she whispered.

I nodded. "Where is he?"

"In the basement."

I grabbed my rolling briefcase from the back seat and followed her inside. A gust of cold air welcomed me. I walked to the couch and kissed Sylvie on the top of the head. She stood up and hugged me.

"We had pizza."

"That's good, Lovie. How was your day?"

"Good. We lost power in the thunderstorm this morning but got it back. Still no WiFi or cable though."

"Comcast says it will come back tomorrow," Sienna said. "But it's okay. We spent all day playing *Kirby's Epic Yarn*. It was fun."

I pulled them both into a big hug. When we went to London together the summer before, I called us the Three Musketeers. Now that felt like a premonition.

The kids pulled away and I walked into the kitchen to find one piece of pizza left in the box. As long as I'd been traveling for work, my only rule was to leave the last piece (of chocolate, pizza, wings, etc.) for Mom when she got home. I started in on the slice. My gaze drifted over to the closed basement door.

"Do you guys want to take a walk?" Sienna nodded. Sylvie

stayed motionless in front of the computer.

"Come on. Maybe we'll see a downed tree from the storm."

Sylvie shrugged and started putting on her shoes.

"Thanks, Lovie. I'll be ready to go in ten minutes." I took the pizza with me and walked upstairs to the bedroom.

What I found made me fall back into the door frame. Jim's side table was empty, and his lamp gone. I walked into our bathroom. His shaving cream and razor were absent too. I hurried to the hall bathroom and opened a formerly empty medicine cabinet. It was filled with Jim's stuff.

"Mom, are you ready yet?" Sienna yelled up the stairs.

"Just give me five." I changed and walked down the second-floor stairs looking at the framed pictures over the wooden banister. In addition to kids' photos, there were a few family ones I'd been reluctant to burn. One had all of us in blue jeans and white shirts. It was from the year after the fight over my writing – another time I could have left him.

Why hadn't I? Maybe because I believed in marriage. My parents were together for over forty years. Jim's even longer. Which is partly why I picked him. Being married was what we were wired to do. In the last few years, I'd given up being happy and didn't expect it anymore. But I knew it was important to stay for the kids. I thought we had an unspoken treaty to do that - for them.

He'd violated that.

I told him repeatedly over the years that if he cheated, I would divorce him. That was something I could never forgive. And yet he went ahead and did it.

Did he do it on purpose, knowing that was the only way I'd leave?

*Chapter Six*

# THERE ARE WORSE THINGS

It was gloomy and damp the day of my second yoga teacher training. I found a parking spot at the studio front entrance and hurried up the flight of stairs to class.

As I sat on a bench to take off my shoes, two large leather-sandaled feet appeared in front of my face. I looked up to see Yoga Rob. "I read your last essay. How're you doing?" he asked. I'd submitted my monthly yoga teacher training essay on the Yamas the day before. I used the yoga commandments to process my husband's infidelity. I bet the one where I applied ahimsa (non-violence) to refrain from keying his red Porsche was a new twist for a yoga essay.

I started to tear up, and he gestured for us to go into an empty yoga room. He handed me a box of Kleenex. After I dabbed my eyes, I gave him the short version, then said, "I'm so angry at him."

"What are your core beliefs about marriage?"

I was surprised by the abrupt question. "I thought marriage was forever," I replied. "I made a commitment and, even though I wasn't happy, stuck it out. My husband's cheating ended it. I'm so mad."

"What if marriage isn't forever? What if it's just a social

construct, and you're supposed to be in multiple long-term relationships? To help you learn how to love yourself and others."

I looked him in the eye. "I never thought of it that way."

"Look, only you know the answer, but consider the idea that marriage isn't meant to be forever."

I was speechless. What if he was right? What if marriage didn't have to be "forever" for me? What if I was meant to find someone else? Someone who could actually make me happy. "That really helped. How did you do that?"

"It's a technique we use in yoga therapy. By examining your core beliefs around marriage, we quickly get to the real reason you're upset."

Why *was* I so pissed off? I guess it's because of the wasted time. If Jim was unhappy, he should have told me rather than break our vows. We could have talked it out and gone our separate ways. And it would have been much easier to find someone new in my forties.

Wow. It would've taken months (maybe years) to process all that in traditional therapy. "Can I learn to do that?"

"It takes three years of training. But the next session starts this fall. You could finish up your yoga teacher training and start the yoga therapy training at the same time."

By then Jim might not have a say in it. "I'm in."

He brought me the form to sign up. Even though I was worried about money, and being a single parent, I turned over my credit card for the first-year payment. "I think I might be addicted to yoga."

He replied, "There are worse things."

*

On a steamy Monday evening, I drove into a large parking lot next to a tiny brick colonial. In front was a small sign with two names, each with "Esquire" after it. I parked my five-year-old vehicle beside a brand-new Mercedes sedan. Then grabbed a thick stack of documents from the passenger seat and went inside.

The room held four large cubicles, each with a different candy dish. I wanted to dump the contents of one in my mouth, but stood silently by the door instead.

I could hear a nasal New Jersey accent coming from an office in the back. The woman in the closest cubicle said hello and suggested I take a seat. She pointed toward the "client waiting room" – five uncomfortable metal black leather chairs and a small glass table stacked with magazines. I sat and picked up an old People magazine with a story about Blake Shelton and Miranda Lambert's divorce.

I'd barely gotten through the "Who Wore it Best?" section when I heard, "Dawna?" A middle-aged woman in a bright blue suit walked over to me. Her brunette shoulder-length hair was teased high in the back, and her spicy perfume gave me an instant headache. She looked down at me from magnifying-glass-weight red-framed glasses. "I'm Amanda Petrofsky. It's good to meet you."

I followed her inside a large room with an enormous mahogany desk. On her bookshelves were twenty or so framed pictures. They showed Amanda with what looked to be her husband, kids, and grandkids. I dropped into one of two leather chairs.

Amanda took out a yellow legal pad and pen from the desk and sat down. "So, how can I help you today?"

"I think I want a divorce." The last word choked in my throat.

"Why don't you tell me why you *might* want a divorce?"

I felt like crying, but held it in. "My husband cheated on me."

"Are you sure?"

"Yes. He admitted it."

She wrote something on the pad, then asked me to tell the entire story. I told her the short version, which must not have been enough because she launched into a long list of questions. I hate questions. As a child, I got Daddy in trouble by answering some nosy questions from a churchgoer. I can't remember what I said but do remember Mother yelling at me never to trust anyone asking questions.

To stop the latest barrage, I asked, "What does the divorce process entail?"

"Do you already know what you want in terms of assets and custody?"

"I guess so. I just want the house, my retirement assets, and my Mini Cooper. Jim has a business and other vehicles he'll want to keep. If I get the assets I want, he can have the business and his *toys*."

"What about custody? Do you have kids?"

"We have two, but one is eighteen, the other is just turning thirteen."

"Do you want full custody?"

"I do, but it's not practical because I travel for business." I felt guilty for not insisting on full custody. But I didn't know how I could make a living without the option to travel.

She made more notes. "Mmmm. So, the easiest way to move this along is to go with fifty-fifty joint custody and get him to agree to the assets you want. Do you have an asset list?"

I handed her a printed excel report and a copy of a recent tax return. She looked at me with surprise. After taking a few moments to review the documents, she said, "So, do you want to move forward with filing the papers?"

I asked her what it would cost. After briefly hesitating over the retainer amount – as much as our recent Bermuda vacation – I told her, "Okay, let's do it."

Amanda pulled out a manila file folder, put my name on it, and placed the tax documents and list of assets inside. She reached into a side desk drawer and pulled out a yellow envelope.

"Okay. Here are some papers for you to read. Do you want to pay by check or credit card?"

I pulled out my checkbook and started filling out the payment information. I was glad Jim and I had separate accounts. Had I always been anticipating this moment?

"What's the next step?"

"I file the papers with the court and your husband will be served."

"If we can agree on everything – not that we will – how long does the process typically take?"

"At least ninety days. Pennsylvania has a ninety-day cooling-off period before a divorce can be granted."

"What?! It takes a couple weeks to get a marriage license, but you have to wait three months to get divorced?" I noticed my fingers shaking as I handed her the check.

"Yes. But that will give us time to negotiate the custody and settlement agreements." She put the check away in a zippered bank bag. She looked down at me over her glasses and said, "Please try to stay calm. Your husband doesn't even know you've decided to divorce him. That's when the real fun begins."

Fun? I wanted to tell her where to get off. I wanted to ask how Ms. Happily Married Forever would know how difficult this is. I wanted to tell her about my anxiety and how being trapped was triggering it.

*Save it for your therapist. Her hourly rates are cheaper.*

I said, "Sorry I got upset, but this is frustrating. Especially since he's living in the same house with me."

"Well, don't leave the house if you want to keep it. And if you ever want primary custody, it will be better to keep your youngest's environment stable."

"I'm not sure how I'll keep living with Jim. At least I have the beach house to escape to."

"For now. You'll probably have to give that up if you want to keep your primary residence."

Tears escaped from my eyes. This was really happening. My life was ending.

She handed me a ready tissue box. After a few minutes, I dried my cheeks and followed her to the office door.

She said she'd follow up with a copy of the papers for me to review. She would file them in a week if everything fell into place.

I left the building mulling over her words. And trying to remember the last time my world had turned upside down.

***

The room was long and narrow like a sardine can placed on its side. Sometimes my gaze would flicker toward the glass door at the end as squeaky gurneys wheeled past. Was Daddy on one of them?

When I felt strong, which wasn't often, I'd sit on the scratchy yellow couch and play hidden word puzzles. The pastime was introduced to me by Mother (she hated when we called her "Mom") when I was six, to occupy me in church.

Most of the time I was dizzy and scared. To keep from fainting, I'd lay on the floor with my feet on a chair and try to breathe as instructed in therapy. Four counts in, eight counts out.

When Mother called me at college to say Daddy was rushed to the hospital, she made it clear I didn't have to come. She didn't want to deal with my medical phobia on top of everything else.

There's some irony there. My phobia may have started with her. Or so my new college psychologist suggested.

I was four when some sort of illness required me to get lots of shots in the bum at the doctor's office. Mother held me down for them. I hated it. The feeling of helplessness, of being trapped with no control. It felt so much like when she spanked me, I ended up equating the two. From there a phobia was born, and I've been scaring perfectly nice doctors and nurses by fainting ever since.

Without fail, each year when my classmates and I got our booster shots or TB tests, I fainted. If someone even talked about shots or a room smelled like antiseptic, I would get dizzy. My worried parents took me to multiple specialists. A particular kind of hell for someone with a medical phobia.

They found nothing.

Strangely, they never took me to a psychologist. And no one ever asked about my home life. But I probably wouldn't have said anything. Because I thought multiple daily spankings - sometimes for no apparent reason - were normal.

It wasn't until college that everything unraveled. My fears had metastasized to the point where I was afraid to leave my dorm. A friend suggested I visit the school's counseling center. They diagnosed me with a general anxiety disorder and the medical phobia. They taught me breathing practices to manage anxiety. And even tried to get me to meditate, but I couldn't stay still and quiet for that long. Not then.

Now Daddy was in emergency bypass surgery. The procedure was still relatively new, so they gave our family this sardine can of a room to wait in. My sister and brothers came and went, for coffee – or rum. Mother and I stayed put. If moving from floor to yellow couch could be considered staying put.

The thought of him not surviving the surgery was shattering. It wasn't something that had ever entered my head. I adored him. And my definition of fatherhood included Daddy walking me down the aisle and bouncing grandkids on his knee. It did not involve his sudden absence. Not yet. Not with me, barely into my twenties.

I'm embarrassed to say this, but when Mother called about Daddy, I did hesitate. But not for long. One fear overrode a host of others. Within hours I was fidgeting in the waiting room - wondering how I would survive if he died.

Then he died.

*Chapter Seven*

# SEERSUCKER

I looked at my naked reflection in the full-length hotel mirror. Weeks of barely eating had diminished my size, yet dimpling was everywhere. How would I ever stand naked in front of another man?

Mother constantly nagged me about my weight. Even complained to our church's women's group when I was eight that I kept getting bigger no matter what she tried. A sneering kid shared that tidbit during Sunday school. I will never forget how everyone laughed at me.

Deb had left home by then, and the only time I ever achieved normal weight were the two summers I spent with her, my former "Mom." And no – no one ever asked a psychologist about that either.

I grabbed a tight black and white striped dress from the closet and quickly tugged it on. Then rescued an old pair of control top pantyhose from a zipper pouch in my roller-board suitcase. Thank goodness it was still cool enough in Chicago to wear them.

In the bathroom, I put on lipstick and sprayed my hair. Even though I was here for work, it felt like a vacation to be away from home. Jim had received the divorce papers a few days before, and

I'd been waiting for him to erupt. But nothing. Which worried me. What was he planning?

I took one last look in the mirror before heading out the door. Not bad for fifty-one.

I closed the door behind me and noticed my hand had left sweat on the doorknob. What if no one found me attractive?

What if they did?

*

At dusk, I walked into the dimly lit restaurant. It would have been an excellent locale for a clandestine meeting. The only light source was a sparkly bar sculpture made of wine bottles. I imagined it saying, "Drink me, drink me!"

From the darkness, I heard a voice, "Donna, Donna? Over here."

I turned to see my single friend Meg in a black shift, pearls, and flats. She had a blonde page boy and was pretty in a girl-next-door kind of way. We hugged and I sat down. "Wow, you look dressed up," she said.

"Just got this. First chance I had to wear it." I don't know why I lied. I'd bought the dress months earlier.

I waved to get the server's attention and we ordered a bottle of red wine. As we waited for his return, we caught up on work. Meg still had the same job. I'd moved twice since we last met.

Even though I always did well at work, at some point I would grow frustrated with the job, or my boss, or how they were managing the company, and I would leave. I did this over and over. And never wondered if it was me – not the place – that was to blame.

The waiter came with the wine and poured our glasses. When he left, we clinked and took a sip, which gave me the courage to say, "I'm getting a divorce."

"Oh, that explains the sexy non-work dress on a Wednesday."

I laughed. Meg asked what happened, and over wine and the eventual charcuterie plate, I told her. If she was surprised, she hid it well. When the bottle was finished, she said, "Want to go bar hopping?"

My eyes opened wide, and I covered the smile on my face with my hand. "If you want to. I know it's a *school* night."

She waved me off, "No worries. This'll be fun."

We paid the bill and took a cab to a skyscraper downtown. We rode the elevator to the rooftop bar, found a standing table facing the lake sunset, and ordered drinks. The cost per glass of wine was more than the entire bottle at the last place. As we talked, an attractive bearded man in a blue seersucker suit walked over. I've had a thing for seersucker suits since watching the show *Matlock* as a kid. I gulped the last of my wine.

"May I buy you another glass?" he asked. "There's an excellent cabernet from California on the wine list. It has lovely vanilla and berry notes."

"I love cabernet."

"Then that is what you will have." He got the attention of the waiter and pointed to a forty-dollar-glass.

I looked at him and said, "Uh, thank you. But that's an expensive wine." What was he expecting in exchange?

"That's okay, I can afford it," he said, turning to Meg. "Are you ready for another one?"

"In a little bit. We're trying to figure out our next stop."

"Do you like music?"

"Absolutely," Meg said.

"How about the Redhead Piano Bar?"

"Oh, I've heard of that, but never been," Meg said. He told us it was a sing-along bar with music for all ages. But mainly frequented by people our age.

Within an hour Meg and I were walking toward the Redhead. By then, my speech was slurry, so we veered into a greasy spoon for a cheeseburger and fries. We lost Seersucker in the burger joint but found him again at the piano bar.

The place was perfect – people our age, some older – and the pianists took all requests, from classical to modern, jazz to rock. There was a circular bar around the grand piano and the crowd was standing room only. I marveled at the pianist's talent and patience.

A few men flirted with me and I let them buy me drinks. But I was an alien in this dating world. I'd wondered what it would be like to be naked in front of another man. Could I go through with it?

As the night continued, there were lots of requests for Billy Joel. "Only the Good Die Young." "Just the Way You Are." When the pianist played "New York State of Mind," I cried. It's one of my favorites. Meg hugged me as we sang along.

At last call, Seersucker asked if he could walk me home.

I don't remember anything after that.

*

The next day I woke up naked in my hotel room. Mind reeling, I glanced over to see if anyone was beside me. Then the night filtered back. No, nothing happened. I just forgot a nightgown.

I sat up and drank from the bottle of water next to the bed. Years of sales conference drinking and the cheeseburger served me well. I didn't feel that bad. Maybe I could get used to the single life again.

An hour later, I grabbed a taxi to the headquarters of a local banking client and spent the rest of the day there. That night I begged off dinner with a colleague and went to a local department store outlet. I went in planning to get a pajama set, but a peachy orange satin negligee called to me, along with a matching floral bathrobe. They fit beautifully.

I fantasized about wearing them for someone other than my husband.

*

That weekend, during a chakra energy discussion in yoga teacher training, I discovered that the negligee was the same color as the sacral chakra. Which meant I had a deficit in sexual energy.

I had painted a wall in my "she den" that color. Thank God none of my friends spoke chakra.

Yet.

*Chapter Eight*

# DON'T STOP BELIEVIN'

It was a week later. Fourth of July weekend. Cell service was intermittent, GPS unhelpful, and the road muddy and unmarked.

"This is like the opening scene of every horror film. Two new people come to a house filled with strangers in the middle of nowhere – and then someone gets murdered," Sienna said.

"Mmmm," I grunted, trying to figure out which of the two houses ahead belonged to my work friend Connie. Taking a shot, I drove toward the building in front of the lake. Ah – a familiar luxury SUV. We parked, grabbed our stuff, and went inside the "cabin" – really an eight-bedroom vacation home with two kitchens, a large game room, and a bar. More than twenty people were expected for the holiday weekend. Mostly couples.

And I was without a mate for the first time in over twenty years.

Before dinner, Sienna and I settled into our assigned twin bed castle-themed room. I guess being single landed me at the "kids' table" again. After dinner, we gathered in the bar, which had a stage and an electronic piano.

"I bought her that expensive keyboard, but she never uses it," said a man on a barstool.

From the other end of the room, I heard a woman say, "All he ever does is mow the lawn and weed the front yard." The conversations mimicked mine with Jim. Him complaining about the anniversary car he bought me, me about his evasive gardening.

Even though I hadn't said anything about filing for divorce, Connie must have, because it felt like there was a neon light over my head that said, "Available." Some of the men gravitated toward me. Filling my wine glass, chatting me up about vacation plans. It was nice to have the attention, but also uncomfortable and sad. The last thing I wanted was a man that was taken. Or to help anyone else cheat.

Since no one was playing the piano, everyone decided to launch into a home version of "Lip Sync Battle." One by one each person lip-synched a song. The best performer was a bespectacled middle-aged woman who rapped to "Bust a Move." She was amazingly accurate with the lyrics and her breakdancing was hilarious. When she finished, we all stood and clapped.

Then came one of my favorite songs, "Don't Stop Believin'," by Journey (don't judge). I felt like the universe was speaking to me. I grabbed Sienna's hand and we lip-synched the lyrics. I started to tear up. It felt like a battle cry. We ended back-to-back, looking up toward the water-damaged dropped ceiling American Idol-style, our hands around invisible mics. We also received a standing ovation. And now I had a theme song.

\*

The next afternoon, Sienna was learning to fish. I was too – sort of. I heard her nervous laugh echo across the lake as I ducked into the bedroom. I lay on a twin bed and picked up my cell phone. Even though the signal was weak, I was able to Google "dating sites for older people." A link for *Our Time* came up.

There was no intro or "about" page. It just started asking questions. My favorite.

"Are you a woman seeking a man or a woman seeking a woman?" I selected woman seeking a man – although life might be easier if I changed that preference.

"Birthdate." I considered lying, but how can you start a relationship fibbing about something as basic as your age? I typed in my actual birthdate.

"Education." Should I say bachelor's degree in case a master's is too intimidating? Screw that. I entered MBA.

What did I want in a mate? They don't have categories for what I really wanted. Someone kind, faithful, and funny like my father. Who wouldn't yell at me when I couldn't find the door key or dump their crappy day on me without asking about mine. Who loved music and would never make me leave a Billy Joel/Elton John concert midway because the music was too loud. And the holy grail – a man who loved poetry.

I was more likely to find one who lived on the moon.

It asked me to upload a picture. Since I looked hungover from partying, I decided to wait. They asked for a thirty-second elevator speech. Thinking back to the Chicago outing with Meg I wrote:

"Recently I began my night watching the sunset on a swanky rooftop and ended it singing Billy Joel songs at a dive piano bar. Along the way, I met a lot of men, but not the one. Are you him?"

I answered questions about political affiliation (middle of the road), exercise preferences (yoga and cycling), and whether I liked dogs or cats (dogs, as there was no option for both). They prompted me for credit card information, and immediately my profile posted. I was dating online. The process had taken fifteen minutes. I put down the phone and went looking for Sienna.

*

I kept checking the site throughout the day, even peeking during stoplights on the two-hour drive home. Less than ten views of my profile. I Googled, "Online dating no views." Oh, I needed a fabulous photo.

After doing my makeup and hair the following morning, I took a selfie. By the end of the day, I had over 100 views. And messages. Mostly from men in the construction field.

One of my favorites, Darryl, became a dating mentor. His questions were inappropriate (What is your bra size? Do you wear thongs?), but the messages were a lifeline. My favorite was, "What are you doing on this site at 4 a.m.? You need a man in your bed."

I messaged back, "You're probably right." And he was. I was online, filling the holes in my broken marriage with strange men. Sometimes not men. One changed his picture to that of a middle-aged woman after we'd been messaging for about a week. Soon after, somebody terminated that account.

Most of my profile feedback was basic, uninspiring. "Beautiful picture." "I'm interested in you." But one day, scrolling through messages, I saw this question, "What's your favorite Billy Joel song?"

I looked at his profile. He was handsome with a salt and pepper beard, a full head of hair, and beautiful blueish eyes. And his profile summary said writer, master's degree, and five-foot-eight. I winced, as if hearing a needle screech across a vinyl record. That was my height.

Mother said to look for tall men like Daddy, so I'd feel smaller.

And not to trust anyone. Men would only take advantage of me. As a result, all of my relationships had been with men six feet or taller, and none of them turned out well.

Like George Costanza on *Seinfeld*, I needed to do the opposite.

"New York State of Mind," I wrote back.

"I have tickets to see him this fall. I've never seen him before."

I had never been with someone who wanted to go to concerts, much less bought the tickets. Bet he doesn't leave when it gets too loud.

"He will probably do that song – he played it both times I saw him. What other music do you like?"

"Tom Petty, George Harrison, and Steve Winwood." He had me at Petty. I told him how much I loved Sting and Coldplay. We messaged within the *Our Time* site and eventually texted via cell phone. We gave each other quizzes about favorite concerts, books, painters, and (miracle) poets. His name was Patrick, and he was a journalist. I soon became obsessed with looking for the "…" that signaled he was writing me. It was like I was sixteen and had fallen loopy in love after a first date. And we hadn't even met in person yet.

In the non-virtual world, I was watching my ex pack up his quarter of the house and my daughter pack hers for college. I was numbing that pain by putting my best face forward in texts to a man I hadn't met. Even though I was desperate, I tried to be distant. Not the first to message and waiting a specified number of hours before responding. I wrote light phrases about happy movies and books while watching disaster films and reading a Pema Chodron book called *When Everything Falls Apart*.

***

Electric candles dimly lit the room, and I could see Daddy's head resting in the casket. I watched as mourners trickled past. Some left behind the scent of cologne or hastily unwrapped peppermints. If it weren't for the coffin, this could have been the receiving line of any church function. I pretended Daddy was asleep so I wouldn't cry.

I listened as Mother told the story to anyone who asked. She waited for him to pick her up after work. When he didn't arrive, she got a ride home and found him dead in the basement next to some tomato seedlings he'd been growing.

They'd only had a year-and-a-half more after the heart surgery. And worse, Daddy was alone when he died. Unfair, as he'd ministered to so many at their deaths.

I stared at Daddy's younger brother as he paid his respects. Mother told me he'd been cheating on his wife, and they were separating. I couldn't help but resent that Daddy was the one in the casket. Seconds before I was supposed to greet my uncle in the receiving line, I escaped to the bathroom.

When I returned, I noticed how many people in line I didn't know. Their refrains were the same. Daddy had touched their lives. He'd made time for them when they were low. I felt both proud and jealous - because I'd always felt second behind his calling.

When the funeral director shut down the viewing line, my brothers and sister walked over to say goodbye to Daddy. Each had someone with them – a husband or close friend. I stood alone and watched.

Mother went over with my brother Carl. She stood crying for a moment, then took the wedding band off Daddy's finger and placed it on a chain around her neck. She kissed his cheek and turned away.

They all looked at me. I walked over to the casket and placed my right hand on his. It was cold and dry. Our hands were the same size, and the tips of our fingers touched. I stood still and wouldn't have left, but Mother coughed loudly.

I retreated.

Carl, now a minister himself, suggested we turn away as they closed the casket. I remained motionless and watched.

An hour later, I stood under my sister Deb's black umbrella at the gravesite. The rain pierced the humidity of the May day, but gave no relief.

The ceremony was so short. I wanted more time.

When the minister said, "May the peace that passeth all understanding keep your hearts and minds with Jesus Christ," I started to cry. It should have been Daddy saying that. But he was dead.

And I was alone.

***

"Can we meet for dinner sometime?" Patrick texted a few weeks in.

I put the phone down. There was thundering in my ears and sweat between my breasts. I was too fat, too scared, and too married to be dating. And I hadn't been out with someone new in over twenty-five years.

Despite all that, one Wednesday night after work, I put on the striped dress from the Chicago night, sprayed hairspray on my long blonde hot-rollered hair, and took the back stairs out of my office building.

As I exited, I heard the ding of a text, "I'm sitting at a table outside. Wearing a blue suit."

"On my way." I texted back after nearly dropping the phone. Walking up the hill toward Market Street, the August heat flattened my hair, and perspiration ran down my legs. Turning the corner, I saw strings of white lights framing Mercato's sidewalk seating. It was still West Chester – but in this moment it felt like a *caffé* in Rome.

At the end of a long line of tables stood an attractive gentleman in a dark blue suit. The man of my dreams.

I pulled up my Spanx and walked toward him.

# Chapter Nine

# WHAT'S NEXT?

Patrick handed me a large bouquet of sunflowers wrapped in brown wax paper. Peeking through them, I noticed his curly hair, salt and pepper beard, and blue eyes that crinkled at the edges. Exactly like his photo.

"What beautiful flowers. Thank you." Before sitting down, I looked around to see if I knew anyone. Jim and I did a lot of entertaining in West Chester over the years, and I worried someone might see us and ask where he was. Even though the borough was the home of QVC and the Chester County seat, it was still a very small town. Reassured, I tried to stuff the flowers under the table. But the bouquet was too large and the wax paper made noises every time I shifted.

The waiter came over and we ordered drinks – me wine, him Diet Coke. My face steamed. Had I made a mistake drinking wine on a first date? It was like I'd gotten to the next level in a game but didn't know the rules.

After we ordered dinner – him crab cakes, me Caesar salad with salmon – he asked about my workday. I shared where I worked and he revealed that he lived a few blocks from my office. And that he knew people there. He'd even interviewed for a job but hadn't gotten an offer. I wondered why but knew not to ask.

He asked me the last music concert I'd been to, what I was reading, and if I'd been to the honkytonk amusement park, Knoebel's, which he believed the best in the world. It felt like this was an interview with an obscure list of job requirements.

Finally, I'd had enough of the inquisition. My turn. "How long have you been divorced?"

"Almost eight years.

"Does it ever get easier?"

"It does, but it takes a while."

"I guess it will be better once I stop seeing my husband every day."

"He's still living with you?" His voice lost all intonation.

"Yes."

"I don't think you mentioned that before." He sat back in his seat.

"It won't be for long. We're almost done negotiating the property settlement. Then he'll be out."

His eyes darkened and he sat back folding his hands on his lap. The waitress came with our food and the conversation halted while we ate. I noticed he liked to stack food on his bread, each mound aligned before entering his mouth.

"Did you like the salmon?" he asked, motioning to my plate, which was still a third filled.

"Oh, yes. Just a little full." What I didn't say was I rarely cleaned my plate when eating in public.

When the waitress came to clear the table, he asked for the

check. I offered to split it with him – and was sad when he accepted. He wasn't that into me.

After the waiter walked away with the payment, Patrick placed his napkin on the table and asked, "Do you want to get gelato?"

Although I rarely wasted sugar calories on anything but wine, I agreed. And was glad for the reprieve.

We walked to D'Ascenzo's Gelato. It was nestled in a storefront so small you could only sit outside. Patrick got cherry chocolate and I picked the chocolate salted caramel. We sat at a small two-top table on the brick sidewalk.

He asked no more questions, and the silences lengthened. Silences made me nervous, so I tried to cram them with small talk, but it seemed like he'd shut down. I'd always wanted someone quiet like my father. But this man's stillness made my whirling thoughts roar.

Finally, I asked, "What's next?"

"What do you mean?"

"With us."

He paused, then said, "You're going through a lot of transitions…"

I quickly cut him off. "That's not my fault. It isn't fair to hold that against me."

He didn't reply.

Enough already. I got up and threw away the empty cup in a nearby trashcan. "I'd better get home to my daughter."

He offered to walk me to my car. I shrugged and agreed.

We walked a couple of blocks to the parking garage. Patrick followed me down the smelly, dirty stairs to the lower level. When we reached the driver's side door, I turned to look at him. This was the man I'd dreamed of. Suddenly, inexplicably, I wanted to kiss him. After twenty-some years, *he* was going to be my "first kiss."

I darted in, found his lips, and touched them with mine. Although it only took a second, something between us shifted. I looked at his face hoping to see a transformation, like in the movies, but it was silent now too.

Embarrassed, I pulled away and hopped into my car.

As I drove from the garage into the still sunny street, I looked back in the rear-view mirror. Patrick was standing there, waving.

*

I was relieved the next morning to see a text from Patrick. And more during the day. Our messaging was as frequent as before. Maybe it had gone better than I thought? I mentioned that I was going to see Connie sing at a local country music bar that Friday. She was there with her ex-husband's band. Her harmonious divorce was something I aspired to.

Patrick offered to meet me at the bar. When we sat down with Connie's band friends, I didn't know many people. It felt awkward introducing him, because I was still married. And later when Patrick asked me to dance, I refused. I couldn't imagine being that close to someone in public. And couldn't drink wine to calm my nerves because he was only having Diet Cokes.

We left after the second set.

After we walked to my car, I turned to say goodbye and he kissed me. I leaned into him, and my hand drifted through his curly hair. The other grazed his back. When his tongue entered my mouth, everything tingled. For a moment nothing else mattered. Then the sound of a door slam pushed us apart. I fell back into the car and looked at him.

"Good night, beautiful Donna." His voice was melodic and charming.

I smiled and said good night. As I drove away, he waved at me from the parking lot. He was smiling.

*

Since Patrick lived close to my office, I began stopping after work to sit on his white and grey porch and "talk." We couldn't go inside because he had students renting rooms and an adorable dancing Irish setter named Samson that whined every time we kissed.

I knew why the dog was green-eyed. Patrick made me happy and calm too. It felt like we were destined to meet. I imagined a life with him. Living in his century-old twin – reading poetry on the porch on cool summer evenings.

His post-divorce life gave me hope that I would survive. My ex stories made him scared that I might change my mind. So did my reluctance to be seen with him or to introduce him to my friends. Instead, we continued to meet on his porch, where I could escape my life.

*

A week later, I was sitting in my car outside Patrick's house after work. I had taken Sienna to college the weekend before and she called because she was homesick. We were both sobbing. Patrick sat on the porch, playing "Words with Friends" on his phone. I'd been thinking of asking him to be friends on the app but was worried he'd say no.

After fifteen minutes I hung up and walked onto the porch for that night's "date." "You're seeing the worst of me," I said.

He looked up at my blotchy face and summer-fizzled hair and nodded. Then gestured for me to sit next to him on the worn loveseat.

*

The last week in August, Jim took Sylvie to the shore, and I asked Patrick to come to my house for dinner. He refused. I told him it wasn't fair that I kept coming to his house and he didn't come to mine. He insisted it wasn't right for him to visit my house while my husband lived there. I kept pushing. He kept refusing. I became more insistent.

So did he.

*

As my combined birthday and anniversary weekend loomed in early September, I became more and more anxious. When picking a wedding date, I'd thought that if I tied the two events together, Jim wouldn't forget both. I was wrong. And when he did remember, Sienna usually bought my birthday and anniversary cards. The one year she didn't buy them, the card I received began with, "For the man I married…"

On this birthday, though, Patrick sent a beautiful bouquet of white flowers to my office. After work, some co-workers had a cake for me. Without my ex to remind them, both of my kids forgot, so the flowers and cake meant everything to me.

*

My plan for the actual anniversary was to take Patrick to see Connie's band play at a local winery. Afterward, Connie and I were going on a girls trip to her cabin.

When I met Patrick at the winery, I omitted the fact that it was my anniversary. Or that I wanted him to fill the abyss left by a twenty-three-year marriage. What I did do was drink three glasses of wine in an hour while he drank a can of ginger ale.

When I tried to hold his hand, he pulled away. I tried to talk but he couldn't hear me over the band. When they finished playing, silence descended. He walked me to Connie's car. I kissed him passionately because everyone was watching. He barely responded.

As Connie and I drove up to the Poconos, we drank wine from the bottle while singing along to brokenhearted Sara Bareilles love songs. When we got to the cabin, I sat in the basement bar drinking shots. Sometimes with others, sometimes alone. Later I played kickball by the lake.

I'm lucky I didn't fall in.

*

The sun was rising over the fog-shrouded lake when I called Patrick. I rarely called, and never that early, so he was concerned. When I admitted to being hungover, he quickly made an excuse and hung up. I texted him later, but he didn't answer. Maybe it was the lack of reception at the cabin? But when I arrived home later, he still hadn't replied.

I pulled my suitcase into the kitchen and called him. "Why haven't you answered my texts?"

"I've been swamped today."

"You're always busy, but never too busy to text. It's more than that."

He paused and I held my breath. "I think we should slow this down." He said I was going through too many transitions. That I was still married. Which was infuriating because I was doing everything to change that.

We went back and forth, and I got more and more irritated. Why was he giving up on us? Eventually, I said, "Would you prefer we don't see each other 'til I'm divorced?"

"That might be better," Patrick said, much quicker than I liked.

I laid down on the couch and curled into a ball. "Okay."

"Take care."

I hung up feeling both devastated and furious. He was like a ride I'd waited forever to go on but lacked some necessary boarding requirement. I deleted all his texts and contact information from my phone.

If he couldn't love me at my worst, forget him.

*

That night Sienna called and I told her how disappointed I was that neither she nor her sister had done anything for my birthday. Then cried hysterically about everything – including the breakup with Patrick.

I said I wasn't sure I wanted to live anymore. I don't really think I meant it – but I must have been convincing because Sienna took a bus home from college the following weekend.

When she got home, she said she'd never seen me this way. Not even after I discovered her father's cheating. She was right. I hadn't been in love with Jim anymore, so the cut of the loss wasn't as deep. When I realized how scared she was, I knew my reaction wasn't good.

I resolved to stop dating and focus on work and finalizing the divorce. Everything else could wait.

*

For the next two weeks, I frantically negotiated custody and settlement agreements. The last sticking points were the tan sectional from the shore condo (I wanted to keep it) and how quickly Jim would leave our primary residence once the agreements were signed (not soon enough).

Our home felt like purgatory. Jim didn't leave the main floor until 9 p.m. most nights, so I would stay away until then. Before, I had gone to Patrick's porch. Now I had to find new places to burrow.

Preferably where there was free wireless. At one point, I was so frustrated at the slow divorce process that I said to my lawyer, "Find the straightest line from where we are now to a divorce decree. I can't spend any more time in Panera Bread!" Too many carbs.

When the papers were finalized, I thought about reaching out to Patrick. But I had deleted his contact information *and* he had rejected me. Back to *Our Time*, with a vengeance. At my peak, I had four dates in one week.

I met most men at the Four Dogs Restaurant. It had outside seating, which provided an easy exit if needed. I often wondered what the restaurant's hostess thought of this middle-aged woman meeting a different man every night. So, I kept wearing different dresses, even though each man was new to me.

At the end of most dates the men would try to kiss me. If you could call it that. It felt like I was being chewed on. Can no one kiss anymore?

Even worse, I was starting to miss sex – I'd even forgotten what it was like. Something (or one) would need to be done, to help me remember.

*Chapter Ten*

# YOU'RE IN LUCK

The long-awaited email popped into my inbox a few weeks later while I was on a plane heading to Chicago. The divorce papers were signed and the only thing left was the court processing. What a relief.

I texted Hope the news and she immediately texted back, "Hurray!" We scheduled a watch party of *Million Dollar Listing* to celebrate.

A voice came over the airplane loudspeaker saying takeoff was delayed fifteen minutes. I swiped through my phone and drifted onto the *Our Time* feed. Looking through the list of men who liked my profile, one caught my eye. He was a teacher with a master's degree. And his profile stated he loved to cook for his children and was proud of being a good dad. He also wanted to be a good person, and at times that was tough. I was touched by the honesty in his post and could relate to what he said. I could have written it myself.

As the pilot asked the crew to prepare for takeoff, I messaged, "What do you like to cook for your kids?"

When I landed, I saw his reply, "Cheesesteak egg rolls. They love them." Aw, how sweet.

We messaged back and forth throughout the day. He asked what I thought a perfect date would be. I was walking through Millennium Park on the way to a client meeting, so I described how the round metal sculpture there reflected images. He agreed that sounded like a great date place. He said he'd like to take me to the Hagley Museum. The gallery, library, and grounds in Wilmington include a firearm showcase and the first residence of the DuPont family. I was not much of a gun or history buff, but I hadn't been there with Jim. It sounded wonderful.

We were still messaging back and forth when I arrived at my client's office. When the executive came to collect me, I got so distracted that I threw my phone into my purse without locking it. Unfortunately, the work message I'd been reading got forwarded to the entire global sales team. And I added the following to it: "dlkskjsblbkjgbjs."

I didn't realize my mistake until I got out of the meeting, and quickly apologized to the email sender and my boss. He wasn't pleased, but my co-workers thought it was hilarious.

As I headed to the airport for the flight back home, the teacher messaged me, "What do you want from this? Are you just passing time or looking for a relationship?"

I fell back into the taxi seat. No one online dating or in life had ever asked me something so vulnerable, so real. I quickly messaged back, "I want to find a friend and maybe eventually a person I can grow old with. What do you want?"

"I want a partner to share my life. I have three young kids at home, so before we go any further, you need to let me know if you can handle that."

I felt terrible for him. He must have been burnt before to be so blunt. "You're in luck. I just sent my oldest off to college and have a teenager at home. I'm still in kid mode and miss having a full house."

"Okay, what's your number? I prefer talking to writing."

An emotionally available man who would rather talk than text, puts his kids first, and loves to cook? I messaged him my number and within minutes, Mario called. His voice was layered and expressive like a comedian from Jersey. But he was from Delaware and proud of it.

I sat at my favorite airport restaurant and ordered a margarita, guacamole, and chips. We shared our likes in movies (*Singing in the Rain, His Gal Friday*) and music. Which eventually led to our children and how we got to this point. Turns out we both were waiting for final divorce documents to be signed. He was moving out of his house, and my husband was leaving mine. We kept talking over each other; there were no silences.

I had to board the plane back to Philadelphia so we ended the call. When I landed, there was a text asking if I could let him know I'd arrived. It was the first time anyone had ever done that. I told him I'd made it home safely. That everything was wonderful.

And it was.

*

At yoga therapy training that weekend, we were given a form that looked like a magazine quiz. It was called "The Five Paths to Yoga Assessment." The five paths were Knowledge (Jana), Psychology (Raja), Health/Energy (Tantra), Love (Bhakti), and Work (Karma). Each question asked if you were more like a statement or less. My results leaned toward the knowledge and work paths. This wasn't surprising as all I wanted to do was sit in Yoga Rob's sessions and listen to him quote Patanjali's sutras (yoga's guide to life) and the Bhagavad Gita (an ancient spiritual tale which details the meaning of life).

I had less affinity for the love and health statements. And when we broke out into groups, it was hard for me not to look down on those aligned with the Bhakti or Love path. They seemed illogical and their wish to give without thought to themselves seemed ill-advised at best. As for the energy path – I didn't even understand what that meant. Sienna was very sensitive to peoples' feelings and even had premonitions of future events. But I didn't get that gene. I couldn't sense energy in a room and had no idea what I was giving off to others.

That too would change.

*

Mario and I spent the next several days messaging and talking by phone. Finally, he asked to meet for dinner. I happily accepted the invitation, but we couldn't get together for over a week because of travel and other conflicts.

He told me to select a place where I would feel comfortable. Because Mario was a history teacher, I picked The Gables Restaurant, which has a beautiful colonial cobblestone courtyard. I also found a 1950s looking polka-dotted dress (think *Mad Men*) that I hoped he'd find attractive. Despite these preparations, I was nervous.

I arrived first to an almost empty restaurant and sat at a table at the end of the bar. The banquette seating was tufted with worn velvet fabric, and the wide plank wood floor looked original.

Meeting someone for the first time at a restaurant can be awkward. It's clear to everyone that you're involved in a meet-up since neither of you knows exactly what the other looks like. Profile photos can lie, after all. I held my glass of cabernet steady with both hands and hoped our awkwardness wouldn't be obvious to everyone.

The door opened. I looked up and put my wine glass down.

# PART TWO

## Bhakti

"We can only love others as much as we love ourselves."
*The Gifts of Imperfection* by Brené Brown

*Chapter Eleven*

# WE MEET UP AT PLACES

I saw a silver-haired man with a beard by the hostess stand. He looked exactly like Mario's picture on *Our Time*. He said something to the hostess, then looked down the empty bar at me. He smiled the same naughty grin from his profile. My stomach flipped. I gave him a little wave and smiled back.

He launched toward me like he owned the place. Then without a word, he leaned in to kiss me. Our lips stayed together for a moment - then he pulled away. He said hi.

I must have said something. But all I remember is this magnetic force pulling me to stand and follow him. As we waited for the hostess to find our table in the reservation system, I leaned into his shoulder with inexplicable familiarity. She looked up and grinned, then showed us to a table in the covered courtyard.

He ordered crab cakes and I requested my typical Caesar salad with salmon. We both ordered drinks, but he barely drank his. Later I would learn he asked for it to make me feel comfortable. He didn't drink.

When the entrees came, he served me the salad and some of his crab cake as if he were the waiter. There were few other diners in the restaurant, so I doubt anyone saw when he took my hand. He only let it go to emphasize his stories. One was about the successful high school teaching program he'd developed using WWII memorabilia.

At one point, he looked down at his hands and said, "You know what they say - the only way to silence an Italian is to hold his hand." He turned one of mine palm down and kissed the back. Then leaned in to kiss my lips. I was happy that the restaurant had cleared out.

"I've never felt or acted this way before. My family calls me a prude because I barely hold hands," he said.

"I've never felt so comfortable, and I certainly haven't kissed like this on a first date."

"Let's give this a chance, and not see anyone else until we figure out where this is going."

I paused for a moment. Part of me knew this was too fast. But it felt magical. Like we'd known each other in a past life, and I didn't even believe in that then.

Mother said never to trust people. Yet here I was, wanting to crawl inside the warmth of this man. "Yes. There's something here."

I no longer believed in forever, but knew I wanted to try a present with Mario.

*

Rain poured outside, which led us to linger over dessert and coffee. But eventually, the vacuuming restaurant staff signaled the evening's end. We ran to our cars, and he hugged me. I felt safe and connected – especially when he leaned back and picked me up. I protested that he would hurt his back (not knowing then how right I was) but loved feeling weightless in his arms.

Kissing goodbye in the pouring rain felt like a scene from an old movie. I got into my car and rolled down the window to kiss him goodbye. His face was thoroughly drenched, mine merely splattered.

"Drive carefully, *mio caro*," he said. "I've waited over fifty years to find you. I don't want to lose you now."

I nodded and drove away feeling alive, happy, and grounded. I hadn't thought it possible, but here I was, falling in love again.

*

Walking into the family room after work that Friday, I heard Sylvie say from her computer desk, "What's for dinner?" She was wearing a Flash comic book t-shirt and black gym shorts.

I kissed her on the head and asked, "Pizza night?"

She looked up at me questioningly.

"Oh, right. Yes, you can get a cheeseburger and fries instead."

"Thanks, Mom."

I walked into the kitchen to put my lunch bag and purse down. Sienna, home from college for the weekend, came downstairs to join me. She was wearing a Pitt sweatshirt over yoga pants, and her hair was up in a high ponytail. Her makeup looked more prominent than before. I wondered what else had changed.

"Can I get a pair of Hunter boots?" she asked.

"Maybe. Is your Dad home?" She said he was out for the night. I was relieved yet wondered where he had gone. And if he was seeing that Daniella again.

When the food arrived, we ate at the kitchen table while watching an Iron Man movie on TV. The kids mentioned decorating their rooms at Dad's new place – and the new Pottery Barn furniture they were getting. I resented not being involved. And not *just* because I loved decorating. Even considered starting my own design business at one point.

Within what seemed like minutes, we were washing dishes and putting the ketchup away. Before the kids could leave for their separate rooms I said, "Game night?" They reluctantly grunted assent.

I grabbed the "Cards Against Humanity" set from the bookshelf in the family room and began going through the white cards to take out any that were too embarrassing. Sienna offered to help.

We shuffled through the cards, and I waded into the silence, "Are you dating anyone?"

"We don't date, Mom. We meet up at places."

"Make sure you're careful. And don't go anywhere alone with a guy."

"I know, Mom. I'm not even interested in men after what happened with you and Dad."

I ignored the last part, although it made me sad and guilty. "And make sure if you do anything, he uses protection."

"We've talked about this. I'm not stuuupid."

"I know you're not 'stuuupid.' But hormones make you do stupid things." I noticed her eyes rolling. I would have kept going if I thought she'd listen. Instead, I asked Sylvie to join us.

As we played, I realized we'd left in a few uncomfortable cards like "The boners of the elderly" and "Wet dreams." When necessary, we explained to Sylvie what they meant.

It was good to have a chance to talk about these things. Sylvie had come out to the family a couple years earlier as bisexual. Her lack of knowledge about sex was both reassuring and worrying. I wondered how long that would last.

*

Later, while on the phone with Mario before bed, I told him

how the kids and I stepped over the awkward and talked about sex.

"Yeah, my dad didn't talk much about sex. He just told me to keep it in my pants. And any mistakes were mine to handle – he'd already raised enough kids."

I laughed, "That's pretty direct." I couldn't help wondering how long it had been since he'd been with someone in that way. And what *it* would be like with him.

Before hanging up, we made plans for dinner that weekend – when Sienna was back at college and Sylvie would be at the beach with her father.

# Chapter Twelve

# WE'RE ALL A LITTLE CRAZY

Before my weekend dinner date with Mario, I messaged Darryl, my construction friend from *Our Time*. After he got his version of foreplay out of the way ("What kind of bra and panties are you wearing? When are we going to hit it?"), I told him I was dating someone exclusively. He assumed the direction things were going and gave me unsolicited advice about personal grooming ("Get that thing waxed!") and positions men prefer ("If you're on your knees, we like it"). I should have been shocked, but was captivated instead. And suggested he do public service announcements for the AARP set. None of my married friends talked about sex. Instead, they read the Fifty Shades series, watched HBO soft porn, and (probably) joined internet cheating sites. Maybe all at once.

I put my phone down and walked into the closet to survey outfit options. This could be "the first sex date." What to wear? I pulled out a leather skirt a size down from my usual. Thanks to the "divorce diet," it fit perfectly.

Now for the upper half. I imagined my *Project Runway* mentor Tim Gunn saying, "Can't be sexy on both the top and bottom. Pick one." I selected a pink turtleneck and a jean jacket. Then added a pair of low-heeled boots. I wondered how long they would stay on.

*

That Saturday, when I walked into the seafood restaurant Mario chose, he was already seated. He stood to kiss hello, then gestured for me to sit next to him in the booth. I'd never done that with a man before.

"I picked this place because you like potatoes. They have this Neva's Potatoes dish I know you'll like."

"I'm a bit of a purist. I only like baked potatoes with butter."

"I'll get the Neva's and you can give 'em a try." I agreed but felt pushed. I never wasted calories on foods I didn't like – and never tried anything new.

We ordered drinks, him iced tea and me white wine, which went straight to my empty stomach. I noticed Mario's hand sliding down the back of my skirt. Eventually it found the dimple in my lower back. Heat flew up and down my body and I wondered was it perimenopause or something else? Either way, I didn't stop him.

I tasted the potatoes. Mario was right; they were delicious. Maybe it was okay to go outside my comfort zone.

After paying the check, he asked, "Do you want to see my new house?"

"How far away is it?"

"Just ten minutes." I knew that was a stretch. He lived in Newark, Delaware, at least fifteen or twenty minutes away.

"Okay."

"I'll drive us there and bring you back."

*

We listened to WMGK on the drive to his house. He told me

how he'd heard the classic rock station on the long commutes back and forth to work the year his daughter died.

This surprised me. He'd only mentioned three kids. He said his daughter died as an infant. The details were tragic and as he talked, our eyes teared. I wondered how this loss had affected his marriage.

I felt like I needed to share too. I told him about my anxiety disorder and medical phobia.

"Oh, you're a little crazy."

"Well…" I geared up to defend myself.

He interrupted, "That's okay. We're all a little crazy."

I looked at him. It had been a long time since I felt this way. Accepted – just the way I was.

We drove up to a house with a little porch and yellow siding. I followed him up the cement driveway, which was cracked and broken. The neighborhood was charming except for the house across the street. Its overgrown branches looked spooky on this pre-Halloween night.

He unlocked the door and walked inside. I followed him into the largely empty first floor. There was no seating of any kind. We kissed – first standing, then lying – on a white cloud of Berber. Which gave me carpet burns.

Our reentry into sexuality went well and I appreciated Mario's skills. And one more thing – yoga training has benefits in the bedroom. Obviously, the flexibility and pelvic floor control are helpful, but even more compelling is the ability to modify your breathing, clear your mind, and focus.

If that doesn't get thee to a yoga class, I don't know what will.

*

The morning after, on the way to the train station for a meeting in New York City, I found a CVS and asked the teenage drug store clerk to unlock a package of Plan B. Mortified, I forked over forty dollars for one pill.

Then walked to my car and called my gynecologist to make an appointment. Because, judging by the night before, this was going to be a regular thing.

*

Later that week, Mario said, "Love you" to end our good night phone conversation. And then quickly took it back saying it was just habit – although he'd been legally separated from his ex-wife for years.

I reassured him that I wasn't freaked out. And though everything was happening fast, I wasn't.

The next night, when he said it again "by mistake," I said, "It's okay, I love you, too."

*

As I backed my car out of the garage before work a few days later, I noticed a huge white moving truck on the street. Several men in work boots were standing nearby. One of them walked over and said, "Is this 37 Macroom Street?"

I put my car in park and rolled down the window. "Yes, it is. But we didn't order any movers."

The man looked at his clipboard and pointed to an address on a form. I heard a car door slam and looked up to see Jim walking our way.

*Chapter Thirteen*

# I HAD NO IDEA

I wanted to stay and watch the move. To make sure Jim didn't take things he shouldn't. But I hadn't been at my job long and didn't have that freedom. As I drove away, I passed Lauren, the head of the neighborhood social committee, Chrissy, the neighborhood Pilates instructor, and Dana, whose little girl beat up Sylvie at the bus stop. They were out for their morning walk. Of course they saw the whole interaction. And the enormous moving van.

I looked in the rear-view mirror. Ugh. They were pointing at me.

\*

When I got home after work, I found crumbled newspaper, bubble wrap, and muck everywhere. My front entrance was missing the grandfather clock Jim's parents had given us. And there was an empty space in the dining room where the large china cabinet holding Royal Daulton figurines had been. I hurried upstairs to my bedroom and found the desktop computer unplugged and lying on the floor – because the desk was gone. When I turned, I saw the tufted brown leather recliner I'd gifted Jim for his birthday was also missing. Going to the back of my closet, I confirmed my jewelry box was untouched. But our office where he stored his clothes looked like a cyclone had hit it.

I called out to see if Sylvie was home, then realized she'd gone with Jim because of the custody agreement. I was alone. I walked to her room and saw dresser drawers open and her pillow gone.

My chest ached and tears seeped into the corners of my eyes. I tried to remember the last time I'd been alone in the house, but couldn't. The kids and I had always been there. Together.

I curled up on Sylvie's bed and let the tears flow.

*

After dinner – a buttered baked potato and a glass of expensive cabernet Jim left behind – I called Mario.

He picked up on the first ring. "Hey, babe. How's the house?"

"It's a disaster. And Sylvie's gone. She's off at her new house with trendy new furniture and her dad." My voice started to break, "And I'm alone." Since my sister Deb left for college, and Daddy's death, being abandoned was a thing for me.

"Aw, babe, I'm sorry. Why don't you come down here? I don't have the kids." Because we had negotiated our custody agreements at the same time, we'd coordinated parenting schedules.

I felt the tension lift from my shoulders and neck. "Okay."

"I'll be here waiting for you."

*

When I got to his house, he buried me in his bear-like arms and only pulled away to grab an already poured glass of wine. He pushed me up the stairs to the bedroom. Two white robes were laid on the bed. One was lighter weight with a honeycomb weave. The other was heavy plush, like the ones you get at fancy hotels. I love fancy hotels. I smiled for the first time that day.

"Try them on." Still a little shy, I went into the bathroom and changed into the bathrobes one by one. I came out wearing the plush one. He walked over.

"Now, take it off."

*

We fell asleep early, and maybe it was the wine, the day, or the hard mattress, but I woke in the middle of the night, panicking.

The movement woke Mario. "What's wrong, babe?"

"How am I going to do all this alone? The house is too much for me. And how will I travel if I have Sylvie? And if I don't have a traveling job, how will I make enough money to keep the house? Maybe I shouldn't have been so quick to divorce him." I knew what I was saying was wrong, but anxiety was getting the best of me.

"Of course you were right to divorce him. He's an asshole." He picked up the robe and held it open for me. "Let's go watch some TV."

Normally I would have protested that we needed to sleep, but neither of us had work the following day. I followed him downstairs and let him bundle me into blankets on the couch. He turned on the TV and went into the kitchen.

I heard the rip of aluminum foil and the toaster oven door shut. Then the sweet smell of pastry and oranges filled the room.

"What's that?"

"An Italian specialty – Panettone." The bread was dotted with the candied fruit you find in fruit cake, yet this confection was fluffy and iced on top. He'd covered one side with dripping butter.

I took a bite. "Oh, that's amazing." I was careful not to eat it all even though I wanted to. We'd only been dating a month, and I wanted him to think I had a dainty appetite.

"Is that all you're eating?"

"I'm full."

"No way. Eat that and I'll make more. Do you want coffee?"

I put the last piece of Panettone in my mouth and nodded yes because I didn't want to stop chewing. He smiled and said, "Panettone makes everything better." A few minutes later he sat and put an arm around me. I curled in and rested my head on his chest, then snuggled to get even closer.

"Are you trying to curl up inside me?" He laughed.

I pulled away and looked in his eyes, "No one has ever gotten up in the middle of the night for me like this. Not even my mother."

Whenever I had night terrors, she said, "Stop bothering me," and sent me back to bed.

"Thank you."

"You don't have to thank me. That's what you do when you love someone."

I nuzzled back into his body. "I had no idea."

*

The following morning on the forty-minute drive home, I heard the song "Like I'm Gonna Lose You" by Meghan Trainor. The lyrics about loving in the moment pierced the fog in my sleep-deprived mind.

I went onto iTunes, bought the song, and added it to my playlist.

*Chapter Fourteen*

# YOU SHOULDN'T HAVE

Sitting in my office a month later, an email popped up from my lawyer. My breath quickened. I clicked it open and skimmed through the legalese. The words started to blur. After twenty-three years, two months, and seven days, my marriage had officially come to an end. I felt relief and happiness, mixed with a smidge of sadness.

That night, wine glass in hand, I went onto Facebook. After swiping for a few minutes, I read a post from a long-married, now divorced person. She wrote that divorcing after a lengthy marriage is not a sign that a person is terrible at relationships, but quite good at them. I copied the text of the post and sent it to Mario.

I couldn't share it with him on Facebook because we weren't Facebook friends yet. I wondered what the proper amount of dating time was for that. And how long 'til you announce you're in a relationship. If you announce at all.

More importantly, when should you introduce significant others to friends? I knew it was too early to introduce him to my kids, but the timing for friends seemed less clear. I'd decided to include him in my upcoming emancipation party because he would have been hurt if I didn't. Yet I worried that everyone would think I was that stereotypically newly divorced person jumping too quickly into a new relationship. Which was true.

I was the person who never trusts – and resists all things new. What the hell was going on?

*

Sylvie was at Jim's house for the weekend on the day of the emancipation party, and Mario and I were out getting food and supplies. When we drove up to my house, I noticed a small bouquet at the side door. I hurried out of the car and picked it up. I looked back at Mario. He was struggling to carry all the groceries.

"You shouldn't have," I said.

He put down the bags. "I didn't."

I turned and stared. "You didn't? Are you sure?"

"Uh, yeah," he said.

I examined the small white glass container. It held a dozen red and white carnations mixed with baby's breath. Someone once told me carnations were the cheapest flowers you could give.

I picked out the card from its tall plastic holder and read aloud, "I have waited a long time for you to be single. XO"

"That's weird. No one knows I'm divorced."

"Are you sure?"

I stood by the door, thinking for a moment. I'd given a lot of men my phone number in the last few months. More than I wanted to admit. But only one had my home address, and I was looking at him.

"You should call the florist and ask who sent it."

I knew he was right but wanted to change the subject. "I can't now – I've got guests coming in two hours." I opened the side door and started carrying the bouquet inside.

"You're not keeping them."

"I could use it as a centerpiece for the table."

"You should throw them out." It was a command.

I hesitated. These were free flowers. I loved flowers. And hated being told what to do. Mario was staring angrily at me. I had never seen him look that way before. I stomped over to the garbage cans and dropped in the flowers. The glass container broke as it hit bottom.

*

A few hours later, I was unwrapping plastic from a hunk of cheese when the doorbell rang. Mario said, "I'll get it," and started walking to the front door.

I dropped the cheese and ran to open it before him. One of my friends from work stood at the door with her husband of thirty years. She was carrying a delicious-smelling crockpot and he was holding a bouquet of flowers. I felt like a loser in the presence of their long-married togetherness. I wanted to shut the door and run. Instead, I introduced them to Mario.

After that moment, I only remember two things about the party. First, I sang loud eighties karaoke in the family room. And second, I ended the party standing in the kitchen doorway, drunk and crying about how stupid it was to throw an emancipation party.

*

The next morning, I went downstairs to make a cup of Keurig coffee and found Mario sitting on a hard-backed brown paisley armchair in the family room. I curled up opposite him in one of my most prized divorce wins – the comfy tan sectional from the shore house.

After a few minutes of mostly silent coffee drinking and Facebook swiping, I asked, "Is everything all right?"

"I don't know. You scared me last night."

"What do you mean?"

"Your eyes. They were cold when you looked at me. Like I didn't matter."

I walked over to him and slid a red leather ottoman in front. Then sat down. "You matter. I was just drunk and sad." Why was I still drinking like this? I couldn't blame Jim anymore – and Mario doesn't drink.

"Are you sure it's not more than that? Who sent the flowers? I've been fooled before – and have the divorce papers to prove it." He'd been married twice. "If you aren't really in this, you gotta let me know."

"I'm in. And as stumped about the flowers as you are." I looked at his face, all droopy and sad. "I'm sorry I drank too much. My ex used to say that when I get drunk I either get horny, sleepy, or mad."

"Last night you looked mad. And you don't need to be drunk to get horny with me." Mario grinned with a bedroom smile that made my heart somersault. He stood and took my hands to pull me up. We hugged for a moment and my stomach growled.

"You hungry?" he asked walking toward the kitchen.

"Starving."

"That's good, 'cause I'm almost as good in the kitchen as I am in bed."

*

The following week, I looked up the florist on the internet.

They were in Phoenixville, about a half-hour from my house. When I called, the manager said they had no record of the sender's name because they bought the bouquet with cash. He said this was unusual. Even for cash sales they took a credit card in case the bouquet cost or shipping fees were more than expected. He promised to investigate the delivery further but didn't sound very encouraging.

Minutes after I hung up, I asked the security alarm company to fix a long-broken garage door sensor.

Then texted a friend to ask which animal rescue she used to adopt her dog.

*

On a Saturday in November, I was sitting in the back of class listening to Yoga Rob lecture cross-legged from the front of the room. Between us were twenty or so women surrounded with bolsters, blocks, and blankets.

"Let's talk about the yoga of work," he said. As yoga philosophy could be applied to anything, we were always tackling the yoga of, or for, something. Yoga for addiction, yoga for trauma awareness, yoga for healthy eating.

I sighed and wrote "yoga of work" on my patchwork notebook. We had one of these two-day yoga therapy trainings every month. The lectures were followed by sessions where we practiced therapy on each other. I already had an excellent therapist in Michelle, so believed the extra head shrinking unnecessary.

The decades of therapy *had* given me some psychology education. I was adept at identifying where people were stuck and quickly applying yoga postures and philosophy to help. It gave me hope that someday I might be able to make a living at it.

Before the group therapy session, Yoga Rob asked that we journal about our dream work-life. I wrote:

- *Little travel: I want to be home more to spend more time with Sylvie – especially now that she's with me only half the time. And I don't want to avoid the man I'm with anymore.*
- *Lower stress: Now that I know about the philosophy of non-attachment, I want a career that's not so centered on results. It's hard to focus on the journey and not the result in my current role.*

Yoga Rob led a meditation that helped set our intentions. Then we broke into small groups to share them. One of the students talked about her goal of becoming a Reiki Master. She said her yoga practice had changed completely after her first training. I remembered how Reiki helped me during that Kripalu yoga class, and although I didn't think I could ever be an energy master, I asked for information on her Reiki teacher.

The week after I made my preferred job list, a project manager position opened at my firm. It was my dream job – the salary was higher, there were no sales-oriented goals, and travel was not required. I applied, interviewed, and waited. In the past, I would have lobbied key decision-makers to get the post. But this time I surrendered the outcome to the universe. If it was meant to be, it would be.

And it was. Within a few weeks, I was selected for the new role. I was thrilled – and a little scared. This intention-setting stuff was powerful.

What if I manifested the wrong thing?

*Chapter Fifteen*

# ABANDONED YOGIS

I was sitting in my office a week after New Year's when a text popped up on my phone. "How's things?" The tag next to it said, "maybe Patrick." I dropped the phone like it was on fire.

I'd survived my first post-divorce Christmas, and Mario and I were planning on getting the kids together for Martin Luther King weekend. Yet here I was having an emotional reaction to a two-word text from Patrick. At least I thought it was him. I scrolled down, and our text history magically reappeared.

"Okay," I replied, using universal code for *You don't deserve to know the real answer.*

"I'm visiting Sherry in your building next Wednesday. Do you mind if I stop by after?" He'd worked with Sherry in the past and sometimes they met for lunch.

I looked at my calendar for next Wednesday. My heartbeat slowed, "Sorry – out of the office that day."

"Maybe next time."

I didn't reply but added him back to my list of contacts.

\*

"Sylvie wants a cat," I said, curling up with Mario on the couch. It was the Thursday after New Year's. Sylvie was at Jim's and we were watching an NFL playoff game.

Mario shifted the heating pad behind his back. It had been bothering him of late. "I hate cats. They are heartless and unloving."

I winced, "But that's what she wants."

"And you think that will make her want to be at your house more."

I hated when he was so blunt. And right. "No…"

"Yes, you do. But after the mystery flowers incident you said you wanted a dog to keep you safe. A cat doesn't care if you live or die. You need a dog."

"Maybe."

"By the way, whatever happened with the flowers? Did you find out who sent them?"

"No." They remained a mystery. The florist had not been helpful. And even though I couldn't prove it, it felt like more than happenstance that I discovered Jim's cheating from a florist postcard and later received anonymous "Happy Divorce" flowers, not to mention the weird precursory email a year or so before. There's only one person who benefited from the postcard and would celebrate my divorce. And it sounded like she was still in the picture. "Maybe I *should* get a dog. But they are a lot of work and have to be walked."

"You like to walk. And you have Sylvie and me to help."

"Okay, maybe." My lips scrunched to one side. I thought I should get a cat like Sylvie wanted, but Mario wouldn't like it.

When would I get to do what *I* wanted?

*

Later that week I contacted All 4 Paws, the shelter my friend recommended, and was filling out an adoption application within the hour. I had to stop and start a few times because they wanted so much information. Where I worked, how long I'd been there, my vet's name, three personal references. It felt like I was applying for a job. And of course, I was.

But the process went quickly, and within days my adoption application was approved.

*

As I pulled the laundry out of the washer, I heard my phone ping. Sienna. Her ride had just exited the turnpike and she was a half-hour away. I texted back a smiley face. Which illustrates why I hate emojis. They reflect what we think people want us to feel rather than how we really do.

I should have been happy that Sienna was coming home, and I was. But I was also apprehensive. I'd told her about Mario a few days before, and she was displeased. She reminded me of my heartache over Patrick. Wasn't it too soon to be getting involved again? I reminded her that I was the parent here. She didn't reply.

Twenty minutes later she arrived at the house. After brief hugs to me, then Sylvie, she headed up to her bedroom and shut the door. I stood on the empty stairs. Should I follow? Sienna and I both suffer from the hangries. Wiser to order dinner.

When the food arrived, I tipped the delivery person and yelled up the stairs, "Dinner's here!" Sylvie silently met me in the kitchen and took the cheeseburger and fries container from my hand.

"Wait," I said, taking back the carton and pulling out a few fries. "Okay, all yours."

"Why don't you get your own fries?" she asked.

"They taste better off your plate." My dad used to say the same thing when we went to Gino's restaurant after his rounds of visiting parishioners at the hospital. He would give them communion, using a small rectangular box with tiny glasses. I wanted to drink from them too but wasn't allowed. Though he would let me wash them after visits.

I watched as Sylvie hugged the takeout container to her stomach, grabbed a bottle of ketchup, and walked to her computer.

Sienna came into the kitchen. "Thanks for the pizza, mom."

"You're welcome," I'd noticed more thank you's since she'd started college.

"Do you want anything to drink?" Sienna asked opening the fridge. She walked back in holding a dark sausage-looking thing. "What's this? Soppra…"

"*Soppressata*. It's a type of salami. Mario got it for me." It reminded him of his Pop – who died right before we met.

She grinned, "You know your mom's dating an Italian when you can't pronounce the meats in the fridge."

We both laughed, and my body softened. So did a previously undetected knot in my stomach.

"Bravo?" she asked.

"Of course," I said, relieved she wasn't going to escape to her room again. I grabbed a glass of twelve-dollar white wine and a plate of pizza. My wine budget had gone down considerably since Jim wasn't buying, and cheap white wines tasted better than cheap red ones.

\*

Speaking of drinking, I was imbibing less overall. In part due to the aforementioned budget concerns, but also because I wasn't a salesperson anymore. No more meeting clients for cocktails or hosting dinners with expensive wine lists. No more making everyone else feel comfortable when I was anxious and stressed.

Brené Brown, who has been sober for decades, says she used to drink because she was uncomfortable in social situations – she's an introvert. I too have always been in the spotlight – growing up as a preacher's daughter, on stage in school, and later, in my sales career. Had I used alcohol the same way?

And now, Mario (like Patrick before him) didn't drink. So, without any fanfare, the universe had me on a journey from gray area drinking to sobriety.

Although there would be pitstops along the way.

*

I joined Sienna in the she den and turned on the TV. We reviewed the saved Bravo episodes and decided to watch the Atlanta housewives. Kandi Burruss was sharing how her new boyfriend was getting along with her daughter.

I waited a few minutes and waded in. "I wanted to get you and Sylvie together with Mario and his kids tomorrow."

"Mmmm," Sienna mumbled as she chewed.

"Would that be okay?"

"I guess. But I wanted this weekend to be just us. It's bad enough I have to take Sylvie over to Dad's for one night, and now we have to fit in this other family too."

I bit down on my tongue instead of the pizza. Once it stopped stinging, I said, "I understand, but Sylvie has already met them, so it's your turn."

"What's the hurry?"

"No hurry." Which was a lie. Life felt too short to see Mario only two weekends a month.

"Okay, okay. We can meet them tomorrow. But I'm not going to watch his daughter all the time. That's what always happens to me with little kids."

"Can't help it you're the Pied Piper."

*

When I called Mario before bed, I told him we were set to meet the next day. I was still nervous about getting everyone together, but also determined. I was tired of sneaking around.

Mario suggested we go to a restaurant in Newark, where kids under fifteen eat for free. "It's great," he said. "Since I don't drink, we can all eat for less than twenty bucks."

I agreed, although I'd never picked a restaurant before based on free kids' meals.

*

When we entered the eatery, Mario and his kids were already there. The oldest two were boys, one fifteen and strikingly tall at six-foot-four. His middle son was twelve and the spitting image of Mario. His youngest was a girl, lithe and energetic. She was only seven. I sat next to Mario. Sienna and Sylvie filled the remaining chairs.

After the waitress came and took our orders, the boys started sharing memes with Sylvie and Sienna helped his youngest with the kid's coloring page. Mario and I watched, smiling. He took my hand under the table.

Once the food came, I noticed Mario trying to ask Sienna questions, but she gave him one-word answers. Mario switched to high school teacher interrogation techniques.

When that didn't work, Mario whispered loudly to me, "Did I do something wrong? Why won't she talk to me?" I shook my head to hush him. Sienna had excellent hearing.

100

"Look, I don't need to know you. You're not going to be around long," Sienna said.

I slammed my hand down on the table. "Sienna. That's not okay."

"Mom..."

"Stop it right there. I don't want to hear another word out of your mouth. You didn't want to speak, and now you don't have to." She started to say something, but I mimicked my mother's gritted teeth scowl. She picked at her free kid's meal in silence. There was fakey cheese globbed over everything. Mario's kids resumed fighting over the last greasy chicken tender. I noticed Sylvie looking at Sienna, and she started to say something, but Sienna got up to go to the bathroom.

As we left, my kids said goodbye to Mario's and I gave Sienna the car keys. She and Sylvie scurried off to our car. Mario did the same with his eldest and his kids walked in the opposite direction.

I grabbed both of Mario's hands and held them tightly. "I'm sorry she was so rude. I don't know what made her say that."

"It's okay. We're Italian. We're used to rudeness and raised voices at dinner."

"Yeah, but we aren't. And she shouldn't act that way. I'm sorry."

"Don't worry 'bout it, baby. We good." He kissed me on the top of my head. "I'll call you when I get home. I need to get the kids to their mom's." I let go of his hands and we separated.

When I got in the car, I overheard Sylvie saying, "I don't know why you don't like him. He's nice and he brings us black and white cookies."

Sienna said to her, "It's not about liking him." She turned to me, "I know you're mad at me. But I saw it. He isn't going to be in the picture long. I had a premonition."

"Well, maybe that 'premonition stuff' is a little off when it comes to *my* boyfriend."

"It's never wrong."

"Even so, it wasn't right for you to talk to Mario that way," Sylvie said.

"Maybe I was hangry," she said. "Can we pick up something on the way home? That food was disgusting."

"Don't change the subject. You need to tell Mario you're sorry first." I handed her my phone. "Text him now."

After she grumpily texted Mario on my phone, I ordered pizza to be delivered when we arrived. After we ate, I snuck upstairs to text Mario. He called right away to ask if everything was okay. I said Sienna was probably just hungry. He seemed to accept that. Then he told me about his latest interaction with his ex, Diana, over kid expenses. I muted the phone and put it on speaker while brushing my teeth.

I didn't share Sienna's premonition with him – even though I couldn't stop thinking about it.

*

The next day, the Three Musketeers were the first to arrive at the pet store for the All 4 Paws meet and greet. As we mingled with the arriving foster parents and pets, a small furry black and white dog came over to us. He plopped in front of the kids with his legs flat on the floor as if in child's pose. Sienna and Sylvie laughed when the dog looked up at them coyly. The sound made his plume-like tail wag furiously. As we tried to interview other dogs at the event, the black and white fur bundle kept coming over as if putting a spell on us. He'd picked us and was saying, "Pick me back, pick me back!"

The kids wanted to adopt him. And since Sylvie wanted a cat, this dog might work. It was way more "cat" than the giant dog I'd initially wanted.

Yet I hesitated. "We don't know anything about him. We don't even know his name." We went over to the three-ring spiral notebook, which housed information on all the dogs.

"It's Yogi Bear," Sienna said. I looked at the dog's description. He'd recently been "surrendered" by his owner. Abandoned by someone he'd loved and trusted.

I wiped my eyes with a sleeve, "I'm a Yogi too," I said. The three of us hugged while Yogi jumped between us.

We signed the adoption papers five minutes later. The kids sat on the floor to pose with our newest family member. Their smiles were wider than they'd been in months.

I texted the picture to Mario. He called me back. "You adopted that? That's your guard dog?"

"The kids love him." Especially Sienna.

"Aw, I get it, babe. But I can't be seen walking that dog. It's a purse dog."

"Don't worry – the kids won't let anyone else walk him." They were fighting over the leash as we walked to the car.

"That will change. But glad they're happy now. Has Sienna mentioned anything about us?"

"No. Don't worry. She'll come around," I said, with more confidence than I felt. I hoped giving in to the dog she wanted would lead to approval of the man *I* wanted.

We didn't know it, but we were trading toys on the Titanic.

*

At the end of March, I was almost finished with yoga teacher training. But had yet to teach a class myself. I asked a friend to introduce me to Rosemary, the head of mind/body fitness at the local YMCA. After some back and forth, she asked me to audition during the following Sunday's 8 a.m. yoga class, one of their most popular.

That day I woke up in a panic. I had memorized a routine but was insecure about my body being on display. The thought took me back to being a preacher's kid, scrutinized each Sunday for any signs of imperfection, including the size of my ass.

Before getting out of bed, I took ten long inhales and exhales, then ten more. Afterward, I remembered why I was doing this – to help others de-stress and feel closer to my father by following in his footsteps. Teaching my first class on a Sunday morning seemed a perfect way to start. I put on black leggings, a long black tank that covered my butt, and my Snoopy doing yoga t-shirt and headed to the YMCA.

About ten minutes before class started, students trickled in and waited with me in front of the locked door to the yoga room. There were about twenty of them. Rosemary showed up five minutes later. She wore pink and purple patterned leggings and two matching tank tops that accentuated her sculpted arm and neck muscles. She looked around for a moment but didn't seem to see what she was looking for. She turned and unlocked the studio, then disappeared inside. Everyone but me followed.

After a few minutes, she worked her way back through the students to the door. Then she noticed me sitting there. "Donna?" she asked with surprise in her voice.

"Rosemary?" I asked, even though I knew.

She nodded.

"Nice to meet you," I extended my hand and immediately felt awkward. This wasn't a corporate interview.

She hesitated, then shook it. "Sorry I missed you on the way in. We'd better get started. I will do the first half hour and then you can do fifteen minutes. Then I will lead the relaxation part at the end."

I nodded and followed her inside. When taking a yoga class, I arrived early to set up in the back of the room. No such luck this time. I had to be in the front where everyone could see. Even though this wasn't "hot yoga," I became very warm.

As I laid my mat in the front left corner, Rosemary began teaching and ran through every pose I'd planned. By the thirty-minute mark I was sweaty and out of breath and ideas.

Rosemary pulled her mat to the back of the room and turned the class over to me. I stayed where I was and stood silent for a moment. Then asked everyone to return to child's pose. To calm myself, I instructed the group to take ten deep breaths. Then asked them to move from table pose to standing. From there new moves kept flowing into my head, shoulder flossing with straps, chair pose to warrior two. There were some awkward pauses, and I could hear myself talking too much and too fast. But it felt like only minutes had passed when Rosemary took the class back.

After the session was over, some students came up and thanked me. I smiled and said how honored I was to practice with them. It was incredible to be appreciated for working at something I loved.

I waited alone outside the studio while Rosemary locked the prop closet and the studio door. When finished, she sat next to me and said, "Well, that was a good start."

I slumped, "Was it okay?"

"You need some work. You didn't take command of the room –

you didn't even move your mat to the center or walk around."

"I didn't think to do that," my eyes started to water.

"Don't feel bad. It's a newbie teacher mistake. You just need more practice."

Even though I knew the answer, I asked, "So, I didn't get the job?"

"Not yet. You need more experience. Maybe start teaching your friends." She stood. I shuffled behind her to the lobby exit.

My mind was spinning. I wanted to say I'd already trained for almost a year and was financially committed to two more to become a yoga therapist. Yet I couldn't even get a teaching gig here paying fifteen dollars an hour. Kraken Donna would have said that and more. Instead, I said, "Okay. I'll try."

"Don't give up. You have the maturity and presence to make a great teacher. Come back when you have your certificate, and you can interview again."

*Thanks for calling me old too.* I said, "That's great. Thank you so much for the opportunity."

It was fifty degrees and raining when we reached the parking lot. She gave me a quick hug and said, "Talk soon. Have a great day."

I watched her run toward her car. Then stomped in every rain puddle on the way to mine.

*Chapter Sixteen*

# MOTHER'S RING

It wasn't until irises popped through the ground that I missed our beach condo. In exchange for our primary residence, I'd given it to Jim. Along with most of our cars, leaving me the Mini Cooper as my sole vehicle.

To manage beach withdrawal, I decided to use a portion of my annual bonus to rent a house in the Outer Banks. I'd spent summers there during college but hadn't visited in years. As I started looking at places to rent in Corolla, North Carolina, I noticed that most had four bedrooms, enough for Mario and our combined family of seven.

I texted him, "Do you and the kids want to come to the Outer Banks for a week this summer?"

After a brief pause, he texted, "We would love to come. But I can't help with the cost of the house. Not on a teacher's salary."

I felt my jaw clench. Mother would say he was taking advantage of me. I shook her off and texted him that it didn't matter.

"At least I can pay for the food. And cook it."

I texted back excitement over not cooking and added, "I'm

sending you links to four houses that allow pets. The first one has the master bedroom on a floor away from everyone."

My phone rang. It was Mario. "Do you think we're going to be able to stay together in the master bedroom? Or should we have an extra bedroom in case they get upset?"

"I asked a divorced friend how she started sleeping with her boyfriend – now husband – when the kids were home. She said she just went to bed with him. No discussion, no hoopla, they went inside and locked the door."

"I guess we can do that. And if there's a problem, I can sleep in the boys' room. Should we take two cars?"

"I think we'll have to, but it would be nice to have one car that we can all ride in some of the time. Do they make seven-passenger vehicles?" I wasn't getting rid of my beloved Mini Cooper; I just wanted something bigger besides.

While we were still on the phone, I Googled "seven-passenger vehicles" and looked at the results. "There are a few seven-passenger SUVs. I need to get a bigger car anyway, so maybe I can swing one that fits us all." I compared prices for the vehicles and narrowed the field. "That is, if it's a Hyundai or a Nissan. And a lease."

"That would be amazing."

And that's how I leased an SUV big enough to fit our combined family. Even though we'd only been dating nine months.

*

The beach vacation went well. And both my kids ended up loving Mario.

Why wouldn't they? It's hard not to love someone so adept at loving. At seeing exactly how to bring joy. Not with expensive material things, but little things. A favorite food (like the

Exceedingly Good Bread from the Amish Market), movie, or game. Or the fireplace matches he bought when I kept burning my fingers lighting candles. Whatever was needed, he would give it, sometimes to his detriment. As if it was his destiny to heal us.

That week on the Outer Banks, both Mario and Sylvie celebrated birthdays days apart, and Sienna (who loves to bake like her grandmother) made their cakes. At night we played competitive games of Spades or Risk (Sylvie and Mario loved board games), and during the day, took the younger kids to the pool. One afternoon, Sienna and I watched *Julie & Julia* while Mario took the kids to the local shopping center. Inspired by one character's line, "I could write a blog – I have thoughts," I published my first online blog post and entitled the resulting series *Twelve Months to Zen(ish)*. It detailed how yoga helped me survive my divorce and find a happy ending with Mario. He edited every post.

Mario and I shared morning walks at the beginning of the week, and despite his back issues, he insisted on leading multiple trips to the top of the Corolla Lighthouse. By the end of the week, I was walking alone or with Sienna in the mornings. He was in too much back pain to join.

And no one commented on the master bedroom arrangement. Although at times I watched an exhausted Mario sleep at night and wished we could be away alone.

On our last day, we went to the nearby shopping center for souvenirs. A few minutes into our expedition, Mario asked Sienna to take the rest of our herd to the ice cream store. Then he steered me to an establishment filled with mindfulness and yoga paraphernalia. I devoured the displays.

A few minutes in, I noticed Mario at the checkout. He and the cashier were stealthily putting something in a brown paper bag.

I walked over, "I always like watching you move, baby," he said to distract me.

I laughed and said, "Nice try. What's in the bag?"

"A surprise for you. Since you caught me, do you want to see it?"

Looking at the grinning cashier, I said, "Sure."

He pulled a cardboard holder with seven votive chakra candles from the bag.

I was surprised. "Wow, that's amazing. Thank you." I leaned over and kissed his cheek.

He hugged me. "You're welcome, baby. You keep shopping. I'm going to go look for the kids."

As I paid for my selections, the cashier said, "That was surprising. Most men don't even know what a chakra is."

I smiled and nodded, "I'm blessed."

*

A month later, I got the nerve to reach out to Rosemary for a second yoga audition. I'd been teaching my friends since we last met, and during this tryout I took control of the room and engaged all the students. The job teaching yoga and meditation once a week at the YMCA was mine! Then I added two more classes at another fitness club. All the while, I was working full-time and engaging in a serious relationship with a man with three school-age kids.

My students gave glowing feedback. They said the classes helped them relax and escape their stressful lives.

That's what I wanted too – despite everything I kept stacking on my mat.

*

The line was long at the Orville Redenbacher popcorn stand in

Disney World's Magic Kingdom. We'd picked August for the trip because the plane tickets were less expensive. What we didn't know was the average temperature in August is over ninety degrees.

I looked over to see my "family." Mario and our five children. All in shorts, t-shirts, and sneakers. The oldest three were on their phones, the youngest two were fighting, and Mario was beaming at me. I smiled back. He was so happy – he had finally made this costly trip happen for his kids. It was their first time there.

Jim's family lived near Orlando, so I'd run the theme park gauntlet over twenty times. I closed my eyes and wished the popcorn line (and my break) was longer. Or that I could go back to the hotel.

Not the family-friendly one I booked for us on points. No, I wanted the romantic one with the spa, room service, and chilled champagne in crystal flutes. Where Mario and I could have our own room, and no one said, "Daddy?" when we kissed.

Instead, we were in a hotel where the perks were nightly chocolate chip cookies (which I had yet to try because they never had enough for our herd of seven) and a tepidly warm gluten-filled breakfast each morning. Our room split – by family – made Mario and me the Montagues and Capulets, allowed only a chaste kiss in the hallway before bed.

Sienna walked over and asked, "When are we going to Harry Potter World?"

"We'll go tomorrow."

"That's the only thing I want to do."

The whine in her voice matched the one in my head. "I know."

"I'm afraid the younger kids will ruin it for me. They'll have a tantrum or something."

The popcorn vendor said, "Next," preventing further discussion.

He asked what size I wanted. I picked the largest holder they had – a plastic Mickey Mouse with a handle. Even though I had no idea how I'd eat it all.

*

At Universal Studios the next day, the highlight of the morning was our visit to the wand store. When the actor leading the wand selection looked around the crowd, I willed him to select one of my kids for the ceremony. He picked Sylvie, and I cried a little. Even though we worked hard to make the time with her memorable, it had been a challenging year for her. Both with Sienna gone - and having to go back and forth between houses. It was incredible that she received this special attention.

The next ride the kids picked was King Kong. I'd been on it before and decided to take a little me time and sit it out. It was close to the end of the trip, and I was exhausted.

"The sign says it will be over an hour wait," Mario said.

"That's okay. I've got a book to read." I kissed him goodbye and took the three shopping bags and backpack he'd been carrying.

I found a metal bench under a shady tree. It started to rain slightly, so I put on a rain vest and used another to cover the bags. I must have looked like a theme park homeless person.

At first the rain was refreshing in the swampy ninety degree heat. Then it started to pour – and I stubbornly stayed put when most of the people around me ran for shelter. I was going to enjoy some alone time, even if it meant getting drenched.

But then the lightning started, making sitting on a metal bench unwise. I made my way to a nearby kiosk along with twenty other people. And their kids – and grandkids. With more coming every minute.

After about ten minutes of texting Mario and getting no reply, I found a small space by a wall and sat down. Water started pouring into the kiosk. I stood again.

I tried to lose myself in the book on my phone but kept getting more and more frustrated. My mind was spinning tales of being taken for granted. I was the one who *needed* a vacation as everyone else was off from school.

Eventually, the rain stopped and steam rose from the ground. When I saw Mario and the kids' happy faces as they skipped toward me, my temper bubble popped.

"I'm going back to the hotel."

"Why?"

"Because this trip sucks, and I'm done. I want to take a long bath and fall into a dry bed alone."

Mario's smile vanished and his face wilted. I should have cared but didn't.

I silently dropped the bags in front of him and splashed off.

*

As I walked toward the exit, there, as if in a dream, a Starbucks appeared. I escaped through the glass doors to find a familiar glass pastry display next to an order counter. Behind it was a bearded barista and a tattooed cashier with blunt bangs. It was like I'd entered a Universal Starbucks Ride. I could be anywhere. I could be home.

I ordered my usual – a skim latte with sugar-free vanilla syrup – and sat on an uncomfortable wooden stool by the window.

I sipped the concoction and felt the sweet, creamy liquid warm my throat. Why had I gone along on this trip? And why did I resent the kids? Maybe because there were so many things to debate when they were around. It was never just Mario and me.

Is this how my mother felt when she spewed those hateful words about my weight or backhanded me when I asked too many questions? Was having four kids and navigating the preacher's wife life too much for her? Maybe. But that's not an acceptable excuse for treating someone you love like crap.

I pulled out my phone and took off the case because rainwater had seeped underneath it. I wiped it with a napkin and texted Mario.

A few minutes later, the glass doors opened, and there he was, launching toward me with his confident stride.

He stepped right up and kissed me on the mouth. "I'm glad you didn't leave."

"I'm sorry I abandoned you."

"It's okay. That's why we're partners. When one of us loses our shit the other can step in."

I kissed him. "I love you."

He smiled, "Love you too, baby cakes."

We hugged each other so long people started to stare. I pulled back and whispered, "Where are the kids?"

"The herd is outside." I loved when he called them that.

We stepped through the glass doors to find our family. Two kids were on their phones, the youngest two were fighting over their seats – and one was smiling at me.

"Feel better?" Sienna said, grinning.

"Yes. Sorry about the tantrum."

"It's okay. It didn't ruin anything."

Her quick forgiveness was an undeserved relief.

*

After two family vacations, I insisted we go away alone for my birthday. We'd talked about opening a bed and breakfast using tiny houses, so decided to test one in Jim Thorpe, Pennsylvania, a cute town nestled in the mountains about ninety minutes from home. Although it might have been premature to plan a retirement together – neither of us was even fifty-five yet – a bed and breakfast seemed like a good plan. He could cook, and I could clean and lead yoga retreats.

We'd spent the day shopping but had to stop several times at restaurants so he could rest. He complained his back was achy, so the brief breaks helped. At one of the eateries he dared me to try sushi. I resisted but he insisted, and gloated when I grudgingly admitted liking the spicy crab roll he picked.

That evening, as I looked at the wrapped birthday presents Mario laid on the Tiny House coffee table, I could tell the boxes were all wrong. Too big or too small, the wrapping imperfect. The contents progressively disappointing. An elephant toothpaste holder, elephant jewelry holder, and little stuffed penguins doing yoga. I said thank you and carefully stored the presents in the largest box.

"What's wrong?" Mario asked.

"Nothing."

"What is it?" His eyebrows raised, and the corners of his mouth uncharacteristically sagged.

"I'd hoped for a ring for my birthday." I looked down at my feet. When I heard no response from Mario, I went on, "We've been together a year. By this point, my ex had bought me a ring."

"Are you sure you *want* to get married?"

"I don't want to be a girlfriend at age fifty-three. And I'm not anything *officially* to you."

He pulled me to my feet and put his arms around my waist.

"You are everything to me." He pushed back a little and lifted my chin with one finger. "But I don't know if I can get married again. What will people think? I've failed twice already."

"It's not marriage you're bad at – it's picking the person."

He smiled and wrapped me in his arms. "You may be right."

I couldn't see his face, but hoped he was smiling.

*

One Friday morning, a month or so later, we were cuddling in bed when he asked if I wanted to look at rings at his friend's jewelry store. Excited, I resisted the urge to ask if he'd used this jeweler the last two tries. He swiped at his phone and showed me the picture of a ring. It had two gold bands with stones in between.

"It's pretty." I tried to sound enthusiastic, but I tend to be pretty picky about jewelry.

"It's a mother's ring. You said you didn't want a traditional ring. And this includes a stone for each of our kids. That way they'll feel this is their marriage too."

I hesitated. It was sweet Mario wanted the kids involved. But what if they didn't approve? It was like I had a perimenopausal biological clock ticking - and would let no one get in the way of us getting married.

"I like it."

"Good. We'll go to the jeweler tomorrow."

*Chapter Seventeen*

# 90-DAY FIANCÉ

The night before Thanksgiving, Yogi and I drove to Mario's house. My kids were in Florida visiting Jim's family, and Mario's mom had entered hospice earlier that week with complications from Alzheimer's. He hadn't visited her much in the last year, so I hadn't met her. He said it was hard to see her kept alive by machines. He said it wasn't *her* anymore.

Yogi and I came into the foyer, and I bent to unleash him. No one came to greet us, which was odd as the kids always rushed to greet Yogi. I paused and noticed a brittle silence.

Mario rushed in from the family room, grabbed my elbow, and pulled me up the stairs to his bedroom.

"They don't want us to get married," he whispered. I sat down on the bed and curled up with the small pillow I bought for him the prior Christmas. It said, "You are my happy."

"Who doesn't?"

"The boys. I can't get a good read on it. I know they like you, but maybe it's too soon." He paced back and forth.

"That's ridiculous. You've been divorced for over a year, and separated two before that. My kids are happy we're getting married. They love you."

"I can get them to come around. I know it." He stomped back downstairs.

I started swiping through Facebook posts but stopped when I heard shouting. Then his daughter started wailing.

When I reached the family room, the boys were standing over their father. His face was pale, and he was sweating. "Enough," I said. "Your father can't take this." He'd been having headaches recently and the school nurse said his blood pressure rose with stress.

The boys looked at me. I feared the Kraken would be released if I stayed in the room, so I headed to the kitchen and sat at the table. Within minutes, Mario had heated leftovers and poured me a glass of wine. His daughter sat next to me.

"Can you paint my nails?" she asked, wiping tears with the back of her sleeve.

I noticed Mario winding up to stop her, and I interrupted. "Let's color instead. Bring over the mandala coloring book." She smiled and skipped away to the craft closet.

Once I finished eating, Mario took away the dishes and started cleaning up the kitchen. I offered to help, but he waved me off. I picked a shape to color and we "fought" over the pink and purple markers. She always wanted what I had.

Soon it was her bedtime. I didn't want to stay downstairs with the boys, so I gathered my things, poured another glass of wine, and went to bed.

After switching TV channels for a few minutes, I stopped on an episode of *90-Day Fiancé*. Within minutes I was asleep.

*

The next morning, I dressed quietly, kissed Mario goodbye, and left the house at 7 a.m. – two hours before my Thanksgiving yoga class at the YMCA. Driving away, I wondered if I'd ever feel comfortable going back.

Less than five minutes into the drive, Mario called. "It's my mother," he said. "The hospice says she's going to die soon. I need to see her. I tried to call Diana to take the kids but can't get hold of her."

"Oh, Mario, I'm so sorry. But I have to teach yoga – I can't come back for the kids now." I explained I hadn't been teaching at the YMCA long and worried they would fire me if I bailed. He said he'd try Diana again. We hung up.

I drove another five minutes and stopped at a red light. Then banged the steering wheel with my hands until they hurt. I couldn't leave him. When the light turned green, I made a U-turn.

I pulled up to the house and ran in. He was in the kitchen talking on the phone. "Get going. I'll take the two younger kids with me to the YMCA and put them in childcare when it opens."

He hugged me, and within minutes, left with his oldest son. I waved until the car disappeared, then headed back inside.

The kids were standing in the foyer. Both had changed out of their pajamas, but their hair was sticking up, and shirts and shoes were untucked and untied. I inhaled, and on my exhale said, "Gather up your coloring books and your electronics, so you have something to do while I teach my yoga class."

"Yay!" his daughter yelled. "Can I take the class too?"

"Not this time."

"Awwwww."

"I can't let you show up the other students with your yogi moves."

She smiled, because it was true. She was an amazing little yogi. "Now get your things. We have to go. I'm late."

*

The kids and I entered the YMCA at 8:45. I double-checked with the front desk clerk that the kids' zone would open at 9:30, clocked in, and rushed to the yoga room. I settled the kids in chairs outside the classroom where I could see them, and entered the studio. There were already four students waiting. Even though I didn't know any of them, I was glad to be with other yoga folk.

I laid out my mat, unlocked the props cabinet, and grabbed two blocks and a strap. Several more students came in. I handed over small rectangular pieces of paper and pens, and asked them to write down three things they were thankful for in their life and three things they wished for – one for themselves, one for their family or friends, and one for the world. When one student looked up in dismay, I said, "Don't worry, you don't have to share what you wrote with me or anyone here." She let out a sigh of relief and started writing.

After they finished, I told them I would have to run out midway through class to take the kids to the kids' zone. I told them why. The energy in the room softened, and one woman smiled reassuringly.

Throughout class, I asked the students to think about what they were thankful for and wished for as they moved through their postures. I asked where they felt their gratefulness and wishes in their bodies. I mentioned how grateful I was to be practicing with them. How being together was a gift. What I didn't share was how worried I was about Mario.

After class, I signed the kids out from childcare. We stopped for gas at Wawa on the way home.

While the fuel was pumping, I texted Mario to find out how he was. He replied immediately that his mother had died minutes after he got there. He was already back at the house waiting for us.

I got back in the car and drove away. It wasn't until I pulled onto the highway that I noticed the gas hose dragging alongside the vehicle.

*

I headed back to return the hose. The Wawa manager said, "You can't imagine how many times this happens." I wondered if any of them had a week like ours. Once the insurance claim form was completed, we got back on the road.

When we arrived at Mario's house, he sat with the two younger children on the sofa and quietly told them about their grandmother's death. After the tears waned and ice cream was shared, the kids went to their rooms, and I listened as he told me how she'd waited for him before going. How important it was to him to be with her. That he'd been there when his dad died. And for several other relatives over the years – the first when he was less than ten years old.

I felt sorry for him *and* was glad it wasn't me at the same time. How had being with all these loved ones as they died affected him? Maybe that was why he was so loving – he understood that life is too short to be a jerk while we're here.

At the funeral I met his brothers, sisters, aunts and uncles. I watched DVDs of family photos his father had put together and heard stories of how his mother and father kept the door open for anyone who came by. How everyone who visited was cared for and fed. I wondered what it would be like to be part of such a large and loving family.

I could only imagine.

*

Mario's headaches increased over the next few weeks, and his back pain made him leave work multiple times. When I shared how worried I was about his health, he said he was fine. That we needed to focus on us.

And he did.

On a snowy day in late December, we traveled to Kripalu. The place where this all began.

And there, in that sacred haven, he asked the question I'd been waiting for.

*Chapter Eighteen*

# MAYBE THE UNIVERSE ISN'T AN ASSHAT

It was inauguration day. The office halls rang with sounds of the swearing-in ceremony. I swiped through Facebook and saw posts filled with anger, others with hope. Soon a small cartoon filled my screen. It showed a woman crouching down with her arms open toward a small puppy behind a wire fence. The accompanying quote was from Mother Teresa. "Not all of us can do great things. But we can do small things with great love."

Instantly I pulled up the All 4 Paws Facebook page and saw they were looking for fosters for an incoming group of pups (I'd been fostering for the rescue off and on since we adopted Yogi). There was one left – a thirty-eight-pound hound-lab mix named Jax. He was only a year old. I love Jax cheese curls, so I messaged the foster coordinator. Within hours, Mario and I were sitting in the rescue center.

When they opened the door to the holding room, a tan short-haired dog with long legs bounded toward us. His tail wagged and he shoved his enormous nose into my face. I was startled and pulled back. He lightly placed a paw on my arm. I looked into his eyes and noticed something familiar. I scratched behind his ears and his tail wagged faster.

"He's just the kind of dog I could adopt. He reminds me of my lab Lucy," Mario said. Lucy had died five years before.

"He reminds me of Ginger."

***

I was only six when my brother Carl brought Ginger home. His high school girlfriend found her litter abandoned by the side of the highway. Ginger was all tan except for a little bit of black around her nose and feet. My Daddy said she was a mix of beagle and greyhound. I thought she was magic.

Carl and I never got along. My sister said it was because he was the youngest for eleven years before the "mistake." That's what they called me.

But I will always be grateful to him for bringing Ginger home. She became my best friend and savior. When Mother was mad, we hid together in my room or the fields around our house. We were the primary targets for her anger. Ginger for ripping up the furniture, and me for being me.

Eventually, Mother had her declawed for her transgressions. Something the vet said he only did to cats, but Mother had insisted.

When Ginger arrived home after the surgery, her paws were wrapped with pink washcloth fabric. I could see small splotches of blood seeping through them, which made me dizzy. When she wasn't sleeping from the drugs crushed in her food, she whined all the time. Daddy carried her to my room because Mother was annoyed by the noise.

After her paws healed, Ginger seemed quieter – almost defeated. Like her trust in human kindness was gone.

After that, I was more careful with Mother.

*** 

The rescue attendant handed me Jax's leash and two big bags of food, then hauled over a large wire crate. Mario struggled to get it into the back of the SUV, and then to assemble it. As soon as it was ready, Jax gracefully leapt inside and we headed home.

Within days I was in love with Jax. He adored walks. Mario and I taught him to play fetch and we played every night after dinner. And unlike Yogi, the lap dog that hated laps, Jax loved to cuddle.

He also seemed to read my moods. When I was upset, he would run around and lure me outside. And when I was sad, he would plop on my lap and nuzzle his nose into my chest.

I floated the idea of adopting Jax to Sylvie and Mario. He could be the guard dog I always wanted. Both said no. Mario's daughter feared big dogs, and even though we'd decided to wait till Sylvie graduated from high school to get married (which was years away), he worried Jax might make things difficult in the meantime. And Sylvie seemed almost resentful of Jax – of all the attention he was getting.

Yogi, too, disliked the canine interloper. He completely ignored him. I called and asked my vet if they would ever bond; she said probably not.

So, I decided to surrender Jax to the universe.

* 

About three weeks later, All 4 Paws texted that a couple was interested in adopting Jax. It was a sign – he was meant to be with someone else. Despite feeling miserable about it, I made an appointment to take Jax to meet his prospective owners. My people and Yogi weren't onboard with keeping him and I was too afraid to go against the wishes of those I loved.

When Jax met his new parents, he was hesitant, yet they processed the adoption papers within a half-hour.

I was ugly crying before I hit the highway.

After dinner, I left Yogi barking downstairs with Sylvie and took a glass of wine to the bathtub. Mario kept calling and texting, but I ignored him.

The universe was an asshat. I would never trust it again.

*

The following day, I dressed and headed to work. As I pulled out of the Wawa parking lot with a twenty-four-ounce cup of French vanilla coffee, a text from the foster coordinator popped up.

"Jax is being returned. Can you foster him?"

Maybe the universe isn't an asshat.

"What happened?"

"They left him in the house alone and he tore the stuffing out of the couches in their family room."

Ginger used to do that. I texted back. "Yay! I can foster him and maybe adopt him. Can I get back to you?"

She said yes. I went onto the group text with my kids and Mario to tell them what happened. Sienna – who had yet to meet Jax because she was in London for an internship – was immediately on board with adopting him. Mario was happy I was texting him again, so he agreed too.

Sylvie needed more coaxing. She finally gave in when I let her give Jax a new name. She picked Jake – like Jake from the State Farm commercial – because Jake was a khaki color (and the guy on the commercial wears khakis).

So that night, I rescued Jake. And he proceeded to rescue *me*, over and over, in return.

*Chapter Nineteen*

# BITING WALLS

With two dogs and four kids running around, the months flew by. Suddenly daffodils were visible on my morning walks, and Mario couldn't join me because his back pain was worse. He initially blamed the aches on spring storms, but he was consulting doctors about surgery by late March. After an MRI and a second opinion, he scheduled an invasive spinal surgery for April.

The morning of the operation, I hit every red light on the way to the hospital. I entered the surgical waiting room and was stressed to find that, unlike the tiny waiting room we had when Daddy had his surgery, this one was big and public. I asked the elderly woman behind the registration counter if I could see Mario before he went into surgery. She looked at her computer and frowned. They had already taken him to prep. When I pushed back, she said her hands were tied. Pre-yoga me would have demanded to speak to her manager. Instead, I stood silently accepting while clenching and unclenching my fingers. She walked around the reception desk and placed a gentle hand on my shoulder. Then gave me Mario's patient code so I could watch his progress on the monitors.

I walked away to find an empty table. Every one had a TV hanging next to it. The people at the other tables were older than I but wore the same scared expression.

I checked my phone. No texts, no emails, no *mi amores*. I'd sometimes been exhausted with Mario's constant need to communicate. Now I just wanted to hear him breathe.

I looked up at the flat screen monitor that listed patients and their progress. It looked like a flight departure screen at an airport, although no one would want to go on this trip. According to the monitor, Mario had moved from prep to surgery. He'd said the procedure would take three or four hours. I walked over to the Keurig. There was a bowl of snacks. I made some coffee and took two small bags of Goldfish.

Unzipping my work computer from its sleeve, I silently thanked my boss for letting me work at the hospital. *Good Morning America* had just started its second hour when I sat down. By the time *The View* came on, I'd drafted a contract and sent it off to legal. My hips ached from sitting, so I packed up my computer and walked into the hospital corridor. The smell of antiseptic hit me like manure on a farm. I put a hand on the wall to steady myself.

Sunlight was flowing into the hall from a window. Outside was a small courtyard with wooden benches and stone landscaping beds. I went out and sat on a bench. Buttoning my coat to block the April breeze, I listened while a middle-aged man in an Eagles sweatshirt explained surgery results to someone on his cell phone. The words made my heart beat faster. I started counting breaths.

At a recent yoga therapy training, the instructor said life is measured in breaths, and if a person breathes quickly, they will have a shorter life. Mario had been breathing quickly lately. I shivered as the wind picked up, then gathered my things and wandered back into the waiting room.

Another hour passed with email responses and client presentation prep. I looked at the clock. It had been over five hours. Why wasn't he out of surgery? Before I could launch into full-blown panic, I heard the waiting room attendant say my name. She pointed a tall older man in a white coat in my direction. He introduced himself as Mario's doctor. I told him I was his fiancée. He showed no interest.

"He's made it through surgery…"

I couldn't help blurting, "I thought it was only going to take three or four hours?"

The doctor's jaw tightened. "There was more damage than expected."

"Is he going to be all right?"

"The recovery will be slow. He has to wear a brace for four months and can't drive for at least four weeks."

"Oh, he's not going to like…"

"He will probably be in the hospital for four or five days. Will he have someone to stay with after?"

"He can stay with me I guess." I was surprised as Mario thought he'd be able to take care of himself after surgery. Maybe the longer surgery required extended recovery?

"That's good. He's going to be on strong pain killers and will need someone to help him to the bathroom and empty surgical waste from his back." I put a hand on the table and leaned into it. What did "empty surgical waste" mean?

"Any questions?"

Yes, a million. But only one mattered, "Can I see him?"

"In about ninety minutes. He'll be in recovery 'til then."

I nodded and shook his proffered hand. As he walked away, I checked the clock on a nearby monitor. The life-changing conversation had taken minutes.

In that time, I'd gone from fiancée to caregiver.

*

I tried avoiding conflicting feelings of relief and anxiety by diving back into my computer and work. Eventually, the waiting room attendant called my name again and walked me through the security door to the intensive care unit. I was so grateful to hear Mario's voice as I passed through.

"My Donna, my Donna, come here," he said. Usually, all the tubes and wires connected to him would have made me queasy, but I pushed through and kissed him on the forehead. I noticed his skin was slightly moist and yellow.

"This is my fiancée, Donna," he said to the nurse on duty. "We need to get married right away, my Donna."

"He's been saying that since he woke up."

"Yes, yes, we'll see," I said smiling. "Tell me how you feel."

"I'm hungry – can I get more crackers? And ginger ale?" The discussion turned to the excellent pairing of the two. He mentioned how great orange juice was with saltines too, and the nurse came back with some.

By the time I left a couple hours later, Mario had moved to a shared room on the surgical ward. And was snoring from pain meds.

*

The dogs ran to greet me when I got home, and Sylvie got up from her computer and hugged me. When had she become taller than me? I leaned into the embrace.

"Did you eat dinner?"

"Yeah, I made a turkey, cheese, and ketchup sandwich. How's Mario?"

"Okay. He's still pretty groggy. Did you let the dogs out?"

"Not yet. Can I go see him?"

"Maybe," I said, letting the dogs into the backyard. "Let's see how long he's in the hospital."

"Got it," she said, looking back at the computer.

"I'm going to take a bath. Want to watch *Deep Space Nine* after?"

"Yes."

A few months earlier, we'd made a pact to spend at least one hour a day together. But just like in the Harry Chapin song "Cats in the Cradle," it was hard for us to consistently make the time.

Today we had quickly agreed to TV time. It felt like a small win after a difficult day.

I poured lavender bubble bath in the tub and lit the chakra candles Mario bought me. When I got in, the bubbles covered my breasts. Jake climbed into a nearby chair. It was like he knew I needed him.

I wondered about Mario's sudden interest in getting married. And if that would ever happen now.

I didn't leave the tub 'til all the bubbles had popped.

*

Every day for the next week, I drove an hour to see Mario at the hospital before work and back again at night. In between, we texted and talked by phone. Within days they had him walking up and down the halls to get the blood flowing through his legs. They said that it was essential - to prevent strokes.

On one of our strolls, we ran into an old friend of his who'd had back surgery years before. He told us how the surgery made him better than ever. When we got back to Mario's room, he said, "See, baby? I'm going to be fine. And the doctor says I can have sex in six weeks."

Aware of his hospital roommate, a thin grey curtain away, I said, "Shhh. I can't believe you asked about that."

"I asked about that in the recovery room." His eyes were bright and his color less yellow. He beamed the naughty grin from his dating profile picture.

"Keep it down. You have a roommate."

"What's wrong with wanting to make my fiancée happy?"

My body softened. I leaned in to kiss his lips. "Nothing, my love, nothing at all."

*

Since he wasn't my husband, I couldn't take family leave to care for Mario, so Sienna tended to him. She was already depressed because her London internship adventure was over, and that worsened with having to dispense pain pills to Mario and make sure our puppyish Jake didn't destroy the furniture. I would come home every day at lunch to walk Mario to the bathroom and record for the doctor the color of the surgical waste coming from the rubber tube in his back. At first, I was dizzy every time I looked at it, but eventually it lost the power to unsettle me.

One day Sienna called me at work in a panic. Mario was trying to go outside in his pajamas. She put him on speaker phone while I hurriedly sent an email that I would be late for my next meeting.

"Mario? Mario, can you hear me?" I said into the speakerphone.

"I need to get iced tea. You don't have the right kind."

My jaw tensed, "What kind do you want?"

"The sweet kind, with real sugar. You keep buying the kind with the cancer sweetener."

"Okay, okay. I will bring some real sweet tea for you. But only if you go back to bed."

I heard static as the phone went back to Sienna. "Thanks, Mom. He's going upstairs now."

I apologized to her and promised to ask the doctor about getting an at-home nurse at his post-op appointment the next day.

"That'd be good," Sienna said. "Between Mario and Jake, I'm losing my mind. Jake bit into the kitchen wall today."

"What?"

"Yeah, that happened."

Our dog trainer told me that dogs could sense energy. If Jake was biting walls, something needed to change.

*

At his post-op visit, the doctor said Mario was progressing well and reduced the amount and frequency of pain meds. He also gave us a prescription for an at-home nurse. By week's end, she was visiting two times a day. After a few more weeks, Mario was able to return home to recuperate. Sienna and I recuperated too.

But some scars remained.

*Chapter Twenty*

# EXIT SIGN

On a chilly weekend in late April, I kicked off my black Coach rain boots beside rows of hippie-looking sandals and moccasins and tiptoed through the waiting room. If we were late to weekend sessions, Yoga Rob would say, "You aren't showing respect to your fellow students and teachers."

When I entered the back door to the classroom, I noticed that the "late section" was filled. Pulling a couple of bolster pillows and blankets to the back side wall, I sat down in a spot beyond the guest instructor's view. I peeked around the other students to see her waiflike form. Her curly red hair was tied back in a business-like ponytail.

Today's topic was Trauma-Aware Yoga. "Abusive patterns repeat themselves," she said. "In fact, many times survivors of abuse marry spouses like their abusive parent." There were murmurs of agreement from other students. I wrapped my purple blanket tightly around my shoulders.

A voice piped up. "Sometimes that abuser can be your mother – so you actually end up marrying your mother." Amid some awkward laughter, I looked over at the woman commenting. She was covered with a blanket and lying on a nearby yoga mat. Although this was my second year of yoga therapy training, we'd never talked. She looked up at me, and I nodded in recognition. Then looked away. We tightened our cocoons.

The teacher asked for questions, and several students began telling stories. While they talked, I Googled the words "child abuse mother" and was shocked to find a study from the U.S. Department of Health and Human Services stating that when only one parent abused children, over seventy percent were abused by their mothers. How many maternal abuse survivors believe their experience was unique? And do they dread Mother's Day, too? It was three weeks away.

As another student told her story, I started writing down the teacher's advice. "Survivors of trauma need to feel safe and in control. In classes, they lean toward grounding poses like child's pose and will appreciate permission rather than explicit direction." It was like she knew me already. I lived for child's pose. And hated when yoga instructors told us to hold positions for long periods or questioned us if we decided to modify.

"Survivors need to integrate what happened into their life," the teacher continued. Could writing do that for me? Maybe I could share an article about it on the online wellness site *Elephant Journal*. Since a yoga therapy student told me about their submission process, I'd been contributing articles and recently signed up for their writing academy.

Would writing help me let go of the belief that I deserved the abuse?

"Don't get stargazer lilies in bouquets anymore. They smell horrible," my mom said after I bought her a Mother's Day floral arrangement when I was twenty or so. I'd been too broke to afford it yet sent it anyway, hoping for her approval.

I was fifty-three now – and had a different Mother's Day remembrance in mind.

***

About a year before the little pink postcard arrived, foretelling the end of my marriage, Sienna and I attended Mother's ninetieth birthday party. It was unseasonably hot for May, and we were relieved that the banquet room Carl picked had air conditioning.

About thirty of us stood by long rectangular tables covered with white tablecloths and plastic flower arrangements.

Mother sat at the head table. She was wearing a robin's egg blue double-knit polyester pant suit with a floral blouse buttoned up to hide her neck. She hated her neck. Her mostly white hair was wound into a bun at the back of her head. She'd told me years before that she liked this hairstyle because it covered her bald spots. That's when I started using Rogaine.

I heard her voice raised at one of our family members – and saw her gritted teeth. I put a hand on a chair and looked toward the door to escape, then remembered I wasn't the one in trouble today. I hadn't been in danger for years, yet still anticipated the hit. Expected it all the time – especially with Jim, who never hit me. Only his words landed hard sometimes.

Mine could too.

Sienna and I sat at a table near the Exit sign. She had just turned seventeen and was looking forward to her senior year in the fall. We were so close. I couldn't imagine being without her.

My gaze drifted back to Mother.

It takes a while to recognize a difficult childhood, mainly

because we blame ourselves for the abuse. Because we *are* the black sheep. We deserve the punishment.

It's not until we tell our stories first to friends, then eventually to a therapist, that we see how messed up our childhood was.

And then, occasionally, we see our children's eyes fill with fear. Because we're screaming, replaying. I've worked hard to stop these episodes, but they're always a possibility. The programming is hardwired.

And even as I began to call what she did *abuse* in therapy, I didn't call it that outside of it. Mother was my only living parent. I couldn't completely sever the relationship. What would people think? And what does it matter now? We moved across state. I rarely see her.

I just needed to hold it together - and get through this birthday celebration.

After dinner, someone suggested we say something nice about Mother. I took a long sip of wine. They decided to begin the "beatitudes" with the oldest grandchildren. I listened as the first few regaled Mother with her positive qualities. Sienna was the youngest grandchild there, so when it was her turn, she said, "I'm thankful for Grandmother because, if it wasn't for her, I wouldn't have such an amazing Mama."

Sienna smiled at me, and everyone clapped for this new sentiment. It wasn't true. But Sienna didn't know that. My eyes caught Mother's. She turned to talk to the person next to her. Our family is skilled at deflection. My mind flashed to her saying, only weeks before my wedding, that I'd never be a good mother. Because I was too selfish.

Now my siblings were being called upon to express their maternal compliments. I listened to Mitch praise the woman who'd repeatedly hit me until I got bigger than her and threatened to hit back. I heard my sister Deb mention Mother's volunteer efforts, even though I'd never felt her charity at home.

Now Carl was speaking. I was next. My stomach churned, and hands trembled. I could feel my legs sticking to the chair. Reaching for my purse I placed some money on the table. I whispered in Sienna's ear. Her eyes widened. I nodded and gestured toward the door. We got up and I said quietly, so only Deb could hear, "I can't do this. I can't lie anymore."

And I wouldn't let Sienna lie for us either.

Mother looked up in surprise. Then watched as Sienna and I walked through the door with the Exit sign on top.

I never saw her again.

***

By the time training ended the next day, I'd outlined a draft for my article. At therapy on Monday, I asked Michelle if I should submit it for publication.

"What are you worried about? Did you write anything untrue?"

"No."

"And your mother has been showing signs of dementia, so she probably won't know."

"I don't think so."

"I'm curious. Why do you think you're ready to write about this?"

"I don't know. Maybe because of yoga, I can feel the effect of the abuse in my body. How my childhood is triggering my present."

"Or maybe now you know what it's like to be unconditionally loved, because of Mario."

My throat tightened and I couldn't speak.

She went on, "He nurtures you in a way your mother never did."

I nodded. "And he's shown me what love should be like." My voice was raspy and broken.

"We need to start wrapping up the session. But before we close, do you have an answer to your article question?"

I did – it was submitted the next day. And after one turn of edits, accepted.

When it appeared the Friday before Mother's Day, I wasn't happy about the title, "My Mother Was Abusive: 5 Ways To Be More Peaceful this Mother's Day." I worried there would be scathing comments and I did get one. The person suggested I was a spoiled, ungrateful child and deserved the abuse I received. The comment was quickly deleted by one of the *Elephant Journal* editors. Bless them.

The rest of the feedback was supportive, and many readers expressed gratitude – for helping them feel less alone.

And, like magic, publishing my deepest shame turned sorrow into hope.

*

In late August, Mario and I took another trip to Kripalu. I went to attend "The Great Work of Your Life" retreat with Stephen Cope. The retreat title matched that of his book about the Bhagavad Gita.

I wanted to learn how to fit yoga and writing into my life, maybe by making one or both a full-time job. Mario went to be with me and to explore nearby Berkshires towns using the Pokémon Go app. We stayed in a bed and breakfast across the street from Kripalu.

There are only a few things I remember from that trip. First is the shock I felt one warm afternoon when Mario asked to visit a small Catholic church in Stockbridge. Up until then, he'd never expressed anything but a historical interest in religion. Inside the empty sanctuary he began to weep. I held him, and between sobs, he admitted to missing his mother, who had gone to Mass every day.

He found solace in the church. I could relate. Something about the energy felt like home to me too.

Second, I learned I didn't have to quit my corporate career to pursue a yoga or writing life. Many famous writers like Thoreau and Emerson maintained day jobs.

The third memory is from a lakeside sunset. As we sat on a picnic bench watching an older man play catch with his German shepherd, a cardinal flew by. Mario said it was his mother visiting. Even though I thought that was nonsense, I took his hand. It was uncharacteristically cold.

As the sun set, we watched in rare silence as the sky turned from blue to yellow, then orange, then red, before everything went black.

*

I saw the Facebook message on a Friday morning in early November. It was from my niece Joslyn. "Grandma is in hospice. I thought you'd want to know."

I didn't respond immediately, texting Mario instead.

"My mother is in hospice. I haven't seen or spoken to her in years, but maybe I should go see her?"

"Did she ask for you?" he texted back.

I swallowed. "No."

"Take a day to think about it."

I thanked my niece for letting me know and filled my morning with client meetings and email responses.

At lunch I went across the street to work out at the YMCA and watch HGTV. Halfway through a *Fixer Upper* episode I noticed a voicemail from my sister Deb. Probably to tell me Mother was in hospice. I decided to finish the episode and call her in my office. As the TV home remodel was revealed, I admired the stars who maintained a strong relationship while finding increasingly creative ways to use shiplap.

After returning to the office, with minutes left before my next meeting, I called Deb.

She picked up right away, "Donna?"

I kept looking through emails. "Yeah. How are you?"

"I'm okay, I guess. Just wanted to make sure you heard about Mother." I clicked on the link for my next meeting and closed my office door.

I watched as the online meeting portal opened. "Yeah, I got a Facebook message from Joslyn."

"They aren't sure about the arrangements yet."

I turned away from the computer screen and looked at the framed picture of the kids I'd used for our holiday card last year. "Don't you wait 'til they die to make arrangements?"

"She died, Donna. At eleven this morning."

*Chapter Twenty-One*

# THAT'S WHAT WE DO

"I called you as soon as I heard," Deb said. "Everyone was there when Mother passed. Except you and me of course. We couldn't get there in time either."

I kept looking at the framed picture of my kids. Neither had Mother's steel-blue eyes.

"Donna. Donna?"

"I didn't know she died," my voice broke. "I thought you called to tell me she was in hospice."

"I'm sorry sis. It seemed like you already knew."

"It's okay. I'll be fine." A reminder for my next meeting flashed across the screen.

"They're going to have the service at Carl's church. That's where she wanted it. Are you going to come?"

The screen started to blur, "Let me get back to you. I need to go. I have meetings."

"Oh, okay. Love you, sis."

I couldn't focus for a moment. Then said, "Love you, too," and hung up the phone. I dropped my head on the keyboard and rolled it back and forth. Then quickly sat up to make sure a message hadn't been sent by mistake.

I dialed into the online meeting, and since I wasn't leading, introduced myself and muted the line. Then scrolled through my Outlook calendar for the afternoon. The meeting was going smoothly, so I walked next door to my boss's office. Poking my head in, I asked, "Can I talk to you for a minute?"

As it was rare for me to pop in, she stopped what she was doing and said, "Of course."

I shut the office door and noticed a framed picture on the windowsill of her and her daughters. They were elementary age and looked just like her. All three happy faces were beaming into the camera. I don't have any pictures like that with Mother.

"My mother died this morning. I think I should go home for the day." I heard the words and knew they sounded strange, too calm.

She got up from her chair and wrapped her delicate arms around me, "Of course you're going home. I'm so sorry. Was it sudden?"

"She hasn't been well for a while, but only went into hospice last night. I thought I had more time." I released a little sob.

"Do you need me to take over any meetings?"

I wiped my eyes. "No, I can cancel or move them."

"Then go. Let me know if I can help in any way."

I thanked her and walked back to my office. I closed the door and swiftly cleared my calendar. Then looked at the clock and called Mario. His last class was over.

"My mom died."

"Oh babe, I'll see if I can drop the kids early at their mom's."

A couple sniffs, then, "Thank you."

I don't remember if we talked more, or when we hung up, or anything until I got home. I do remember being surprised that the dogs still needed to go out, the kitchen trash can was still overflowing, and there were unpaid bills in the mail.

By the time Sylvie came home from school, I was drinking a glass of wine and staring at a Bravo housewife show. I texted my best friend, Hope, and she offered to let us stay with her if we came out for the funeral. Problem was, I hadn't decided whether to go. The only thing I knew was that I wanted Mario to cook for me.

I texted Mario. "Can you make me chicken marsala?"

"Of course. Will pick up supplies on the way up. Be there around six."

"Perfect. Thank you."

"Of course, mia bella. That's what we do for those we love."

I wrote, "I never knew that before you" in the text box, but felt embarrassed and deleted it.

*

The following day, I posted on Facebook, "My mother died yesterday."

In response some wrote:

"I know this is complicated. Thinking of you."

"You must be experiencing so many emotions. I am here if you need me."

"I cannot even imagine. Take care of you."

And one wrote, "I know you weren't close to your mother, but this must still be difficult."

That last comment hurt. I wanted to respond that they had no idea how awful it is when permanently breaking up with your only living parent is the right thing to do. Yet, I understood what they meant. It was easier to heal from Mother's death than Daddy's because she hadn't been in my daily life. But her death was still painful – and I couldn't understand why.

I texted Michelle to see if we could talk. She was able to fit me in later that day.

After we got through the pleasantries, I asked, "Why am I so slayed by this? Why am I shutting down?"

"With your mother's death, the dream of having the mom you deserved died too."

I grabbed a tissue and began to weep. When I could speak, I asked, "I wonder why I was the only one that broke away from her."

"You were the only one alone with her. The rest grew up together and then escaped to college."

"But she wasn't all bad. I have good memories of her. And I got my grit from her."

"Yeah, but you got more of the bad than the others."

"I guess."

"Which let you separate from her."

And divorce Jim. "But what'll it look like if I don't attend my mother's funeral?" I wasn't up to the scrutiny of Mother's church friends, who were sure to know our story and have opinions.

"Who cares? You don't have to go. No one can tell you the right way to grieve. You can make up your own way. What would that look like?"

*

The next day, Sylvie and I dropped both dogs at the sitter and drove onto the Pennsylvania Turnpike. Sienna was at college in Pittsburgh, so we were meeting her there.

I'd made the trip to Pittsburgh many times with my parents.

Both before and after my dad was ordained in his second church, about an hour south of the city. On our trips across the state, we'd take breaks at rest stops so Daddy could stretch his legs and my parents could get coffee. I would get French fries and orange soda at the Howard Johnson's, and in later years, salads and diet soda at the Roy Rogers.

On this trip, we stopped at Starbucks and I got a decaffeinated peppermint tea. Sylvie bought Combos (a pretzel cheese snack) and lemonade at the mini-mart.

We picked up Sienna at her college dorm three hours later and arrived at Hope's house around 6:30. Hope and her husband Roy have a beautifully renovated tri-plex and no kids. Staying there feels like a vacation. They ordered pizza and salads, and we watched *Below Deck* and drank a couple bottles of wine. Before heading to bed, we put the barely touched salads in the fridge. I crawled into bed and tried to call Mario, but there was no answer. He must have fallen asleep.

Hours later, I did the same.

*

The next day, while my siblings and their families were at the memorial service, the kids and I decided to make new memories doing things we'd never done in the Burgh. We took pictures at the Peace Love Donut shop and ate French fries together at Primanti Brothers. After, we went to the Mattress Factory Museum. Halfway through the exhibits, we came upon a magnificent hot-house garden with pink and purple flowers and tendrils reaching toward the sky. Mother would have loved it.

On the way down to the burial site, I stopped at a Giant Eagle grocery store to get a bouquet of flowers. Every bouquet included a Stargazer lily. I bought one anyway.

When we got to Claysville, Deb texted that the family still hadn't arrived at the cemetery. I turned the car towards my high school, where my first kiss happened under the bleachers. Next, we drove to the house we'd lived in and the newspaper store where I started and ended my paper route.

When I didn't hear from Deb, we drove to the burial site - and arrived just as they lowered the casket into the ground next to Daddy. I waited with the kids to the side, holding the bouquet. My older brother Mitch and Deb, and her husband Ron came over to hug the kids and me. We watched as the backhoe dumped dirt on the grave. Carl talked the whole time to everyone but me. Sienna and Sylvie flanked my sides and wrapped their arms around my waist. I felt tiny next to them and wondered if I was getting shorter with age, like Mother.

Eventually the backhoe moved away from the grave, and the rest of the family loaded into their cars. I walked over to the burial mound, took the Stargazer lily from the bouquet, and gently placed it inside one of the graveside arrangements.

"I hope you found your peace, Mom."

I took the rest of the floral bouquet and laid it in front of my father's grave.

"Miss you, Daddy." I let the tears fall. The kids held onto me as the backhoe and the rest of my family drove away.

*

Later, we met Deb, Ron, and Mitch for dinner at a local steakhouse. I picked it because I could get my two favorite things – a glass of wine *and* a baked potato.

Since we moved to the other side of the state after Sienna was born, and they were so much younger than their cousins, my kids rarely spent any time with my siblings. So, Sylvie immediately started playing games on her phone, and Sienna, who gets nervous when the conversation lulls too, talked non-stop about her college finals, even though they were a month away.

After we ordered, my sister slid a small jewelry bag over to me. It smelled familiar.

"What's this?"

"Open it."

I loosened the pouch strings and dumped a necklace with three rings on the brown Formica table. One of the rings had a small round stone encased in a cocoon-like setting. Mother's engagement ring. There were also two wedding bands, one larger than the other. The necklace had been on her only days before.

"Carl gave it to me to give to you," Deb said. "Mother said you wanted it."

"Oh, Mom, that's so nice. The engagement ring is beautiful," Sienna said.

I'd always loved her engagement story. How Daddy, a returning Word War II vet, scrimped to buy the ring for her.

I heard the people in the next booth talking and the clanking of dishes across the restaurant. I smelled steak sizzling at a nearby table. My body began to shake.

"I didn't think she remembered." Sienna put her hand on my knee, and Sylvie put an arm around my quivering shoulders.

Wiping my eyes with a black cloth napkin, I put the necklace back in the pouch.

# Chapter Twenty-Two

# WE'VE GOT TO STOP MEETING LIKE THIS

The morning after we returned from Pittsburgh, I woke at 6:30 to a text from Mario. "Donna, I'm on my way to the hospital." I unlocked the phone to find multiple texts and voicemails from him. The first was sent at 2:30 a.m. I felt awful. I'd turned off the ringer to get a good night's sleep.

Sylvie was at her dad's, so I took the dogs out and made the now familiar drive to Mario's local hospital in less than fifty minutes. I rushed through the emergency entrance and asked for him at the reception desk. The receptionist looked at her computer screen and said he was about to be released.

"What's wrong with him?" She gave me a guarded look. Sighing, I said, "I'm his fiancée."

"I'll let him tell you." She waved over a volunteer to take me back.

When I got to Mario, he smiled and straightened up in bed. There was an IV pole next to him and he was wearing a fresh hospital gown. His normally well-groomed hair was messy. I tried to kiss him on top of the head, but he pulled me in for a hug. "I'm so glad you're here. I was in so much pain last night I called an ambulance. They say it's a kidney stone."

I pulled away to look in his face. His eyes were clouded and he was sweating. "Is it painful?"

"It hurt somethin' awful. And it's not in a position they can blast away today. So, I have to come back for surgery."

I dropped into the leather chair next to his bed. It was too much. The back surgery, Mother's death, now this? I was tired of what life was throwing at us.

"We've got to stop meeting like this." The smile left his face and his body wilted. Before I could apologize, the nurse came in with recommendations from the doctor, with a list of items he should avoid. Including sugar and tea.

Later, after I dropped Mario at his house, I went home and poured four two-gallon containers of sweet tea down the drain.

*

A few weeks later, Mario had his kidney stone surgery and came to my house to recover. One morning, as I was pulling on my black tights in the walk-in closet, he said. "I need some ideas for your kids for Christmas."

I hopped around trying to get the tights up. I wasn't ready to think about Christmas because it reminded me of Mother. She loved the holidays and enjoyed making ornaments and Christmas crafts. "I have no idea what to get them. I can't think about it now."

"Well, you better get on it. Christmas is less than a month away."

I felt the spot between my shoulder blades tense, "Please stop it. You're making me hyperventilate."

"I get it. I get it. Is it okay if I ask them?" They had their own private meme-sharing chats.

"Sure, go ahead and text them."

"And what about Christmas Eve? Do you have the kids? My niece is doing Christmas Eve with the seven fishes again."

"It's not even December yet. I can't think about this now. I need to get to work."

I was about to rush out when he stopped me with a hug. "Let me make you breakfast."

"You shouldn't be out of bed."

"I need to take care of my baby." And even though it wasn't good for him, he followed me downstairs.

While I took the dogs out, he put together an omelet from leftover vegetables, prosciutto, and Romano cheese. It was delicious. I kissed him – this time on the lips.

"You always know how to make me feel better." And soften anxiety into possibility. "I'll ask the kids about presents and Christmas Eve. I think your sister's and the seven fishes would be nice."

"Thank you, mi amore."

*

On Black Friday, the Three Musketeers were surrounded by red and green plastic bins filled with Christmas ornaments, tree lights, and decorations. We had already slid them down the dropdown attic stairs and were working them stair-by-stair to the first floor. The kids were in their pajamas even though it was almost noon. I was wearing yoga clothes from teaching that morning's class.

Once all the bins were on the first floor, Sylvie retreated to her computer and Sienna and I started sorting. Some containers went to the living room for the yet-to-be-purchased tree, others to the family and dining rooms.

Sienna opened one of the bins and pulled out a small pink shoebox with NATIVITY SCENE written on the lid. The old rubber band around it broke, and she set the remnants aside before opening the box. My heart caught when I saw the tissue-wrapped figurine. It was Mother Mary. "Look Mom," she said, "it's the nativity figures Grandma made."

I nodded but couldn't speak. My eyes filled a little – but not so much that Sienna noticed.

We pulled each one out. They were made of white plaster of Paris. She had made them for us the year Jim and I got married. When we got to the Joseph figurine, the head was broken off. *That seems appropriate.*

"Do you want to put it out? We haven't done that in years." She pulled out the small wooden barn.

I hadn't touched the nativity set since I'd stopped seeing Mother. And now I wouldn't see her again. "I don't think I'm ready to deal with this yet. It's a little too soon." I started re-wrapping the figures. Sienna hugged me and went to yell at Sylvie to help decorate.

As they argued, I placed the figurines back in the box. When I was done, there were a couple of tissues left. I wiped my eyes with one and went to the kitchen to get a new rubber band.

*

In early December, a text came across my phone. Patrick.

"I have a book signing at the Barnes and Noble in Exton on December 23rd. Can you come?"

I hadn't heard from him in a while and had yet to see him in person since we broke up. He'd periodically reached out over the years, but either I was out of the office when he stopped by, or I feigned being too busy for coffee. I told Mario every time he contacted me, and surprisingly, he never seemed to mind.

"I can probably make that." I entered the event in my calendar. It was a weekend when I didn't have Sylvie, so I might be with Mario. But he and Patrick were both history buffs and would probably get along.

The day of the book signing, I happened to be doing last-minute shopping with Mario in the same Barnes and Noble shopping center as the signing. When the event reminder popped up I paused briefly.

Then swiped it away and kept wandering with Mario.

*Chapter Twenty-Three*

# NEGATIVE ENERGY

The second Saturday in January, I parked in front of a two-story building with an old mini-mart on the bottom. I looked across the street. Another brand-new Wawa with gas pumps. The mini-mart wouldn't last long with that next door.

After climbing the stairs to the second floor, I opened a door marked "Reiki Center." Inside was a small room with green walls and wooden floors. On a shelf to the left was a steaming cauldron-like fountain that kept changing colors. To the right was a little white desk with a middle-aged woman behind it. She had short wavy brown hair, and her smile was as light and cheery as the pink and white clothes she wore. I introduced myself and she smiled. In a Philadelphia accent she said her name was Maria DiPietro. I watched as she checked my name off her list.

Maria handed me a bound booklet with Japanese symbols on the cover. She motioned toward a circle of chairs in the back. Several women were already sitting there. Some wore tie-dye and others were in various grey, ashy, and black shades. One woman had a long string of mala meditation beads around her neck. She played with the black tassel. I took a seat by the door.

A few more students wandered in. When everyone was settled, Maria asked us to close our eyes. She shared that she was not only a Reiki Master but a psychic too, and called her spirit guides to keep us safe – to share their wisdom. She asked us to imagine a white light flowing from the heavens through our bodies and into the ground. She said as is above, so is below. There were more things I don't remember, but when she finished, I felt safe, secure, and grounded.

She began to lecture – explaining that Reiki was a Japanese modality that channeled universal energy through practitioners. The energy was meant for healing, and only positive energy could be transferred.

She taught us how to perform Reiki on ourselves and others. It began with releasing the flood of universal spirit into our bodies, then placing our hands (palms down) over various energy centers: the top of the head, the forehead (third eye), the throat, the heart, the top and bottom of the belly and the pelvic region. Each time my hands moved I felt progressively more peaceful. When we were done, my body was soft, like at the end of yoga class.

When everyone shared their experience, they described colors or auras. And some felt their hands tingle or get warm. I stayed quiet. I didn't feel or see anything.

When we broke for lunch, I called Mario from the Wawa parking lot next door. "I'm not sure I can do this."

"Just give it a chance. You've only been at it a few hours."

"I guess." But everyone else seemed to get it. What was wrong with me?

I could hear dogs barking in the background. "What time will you be home?"

"It's over at three. So, around dinner time. Speaking of which, I'd better head back."

"Okay, but before you go – what do you want for Valentine's Day? It's coming up."

"It's a month away."

"It pays to be prepared."

I told him I'd think about it. We rung off.

*

When I returned to the classroom, the chairs were arranged in a line facing the cauldron fountain. I wasn't sure what was happening, so I sat in the middle. Maria told us to close our eyes and put our hands in our laps. She started making whooshing noises. Opening just my left eye, I saw her moving around the mala bead student, arms waving. I could imagine Jim saying to the kids, "What's your mother doing *now*?"

Within minutes, Maria's hands were on my shoulder. Immediately I saw purple clouds behind my closed eyelids. They swirled and pulsed, and sometimes other colors would filter in – red, yellow, orange. She took my hands and folded them as if in prayer. There was more swooshing and breathing. Then she moved on to the next person. The colors began to fade and I felt clearer. My hands and face were warm.

After she finished with every student, she said, "Open your eyes. Congratulations, you've received the Reiki I attunement." We all clapped.

She went down the row one by one telling us what she saw during our attunement. She said one woman was a natural healer, and another had psychic abilities. As she continued, I started to fret. I didn't have any of these talents.

When she got to me, she said, "Donna, when I did your attunement, I saw mostly purple, which is the crown chakra color. It means you're already accessing the masters."

"What does that mean?"

"It means you are in touch with divine beings and meant to explain their teachings to the masses."

I nodded like I understood.

*

On the way home, my forehead felt like it was in a vise that kept getting tighter and heavier. Mario texted, asking what I wanted for Valentine's Day. I texted back that I was sick and couldn't think about it. But he kept bugging me, so I told him I wanted a mala necklace, like the student's in class. Within minutes he sent me pictures of necklaces and asked me to pick two so he could surprise me with his final choice.

*

The next day I threw up and couldn't get out of bed. I emailed Maria to ask if this was normal.

She emailed back, "Sometimes after an attunement your body has to clear away all the negative energy. To get you ready for something big that's coming." She said it could make you sick. "But it's okay. It happens."

I didn't believe her even though deep down, I sensed she was right.

*

The week before the Super Bowl, Mario and I were upstairs on my bed reviewing pages from my latest book draft. It was based on my yoga blog.

We had the heated mattress pad on because Mario's back and neck were aching. The heat from the pad was the most action the bed had felt in a while. Since his kidney stone surgery, "things" had gone quiet.

The pages were red with Mario's notes. As we reviewed them, he reminded me of things I'd forgotten. The BELIEVE necklace he surprised me with when we picked up the tan couch in Stone Harbor. The red corset that made us stay in bed the weekend we went to Annapolis. I was touched by how much he remembered.

"Are you mad about all the comments?"

I kissed him on the cheek and said, "Oh no, I'm so glad you took the time to do this. I agree with every edit. Especially your memory of the corset weekend."

"Can't wait to go away for another trip like that."

"We will, we will. You just have to get better."

But I was worried. I didn't care about corset time, or that we would rarely be alone once we lived under the same roof with five children ranging from nine to twenty.

I didn't even care if we got married.

I just wanted to be with him.

*

That Saturday, I was drinking coffee in the family room and nursing a hangover. I'd blown through my two-glass-a-day allowance again watching Bravo with Sienna. Why was I still getting drunk?

Guess I wasn't handling Mother's death well after all.

Mario barreled into the room full of energy. His eyes were wide. "We need to get stuff from the Amish Market for the Super Bowl."

Still trying to form sentences, I said, "Wait 'til I finish my coffee and I'll go with you."

"No. I want to get there when they open to make sure and get the wings and bread you like. It will be a madhouse later."

"Okay, okay. Can you send me the link to that computer mouse you wanted for Valentine's Day?" He sat and sent me a text with the link. Then started telling me about posts he saw on Facebook. I barely listened.

Instead, I read from *The Untethered Soul* by Michael Singer. I'd just picked it for my daily meditation reading, even though it had been sitting on my shelf since the prior fall.

I highlighted a quote about being so peaceful you could handle anything the day brings.

Mario said something about not wanting to disturb me. I didn't look up when he kissed the top of my head as he left. It was 7:50 a.m. The Amish Market opened at 8. I spent the next thirty minutes buying his Valentine's gift on Amazon and reading a chapter of Elizabeth Gilbert's book *Big Magic* for the new *Elephant Journal* writing group I was leading. I made a meme of one of the quotes, and as I posted it, I heard an ambulance siren.

It seemed to be coming from the Amish Market, which was a block away. I looked at my watch: 8:40. Mario should be back by now. I texted him. No response.

I texted again. Nothing.

I called him. It went to voicemail.

# PART THREE

## Duhkha

"Each of us has our own silent War with Reality."
*The Wisdom of Yoga* by Stephen Cope

*Chapter Twenty-Four*

# GREENSLEEVES

Minutes later I was up in Sienna's room. She was pulling a long sleeve t-shirt over her head. "Hey mom, I'm just getting ready to go to the gym." As her head popped through, she saw my face. "What's wrong?"

I told her about Mario going to the Amish Market, hearing the siren, and then the unanswered texts and calls. "I know it's silly, but I'm going to go over there and make sure he's okay."

"I'll come with you." She stamped her feet into sneakers. I turned and ran down the stairs.

As we put food and water out for the dogs, I noticed my hands shaking. "Can you drive?"

She nodded and we jumped into her Jeep. When we got to the market parking lot, there was no ambulance but Mario's car was there. I ran to look inside and saw plastic grocery bags filled with food. No Mario.

"Maybe he went back for something," Sienna suggested. We rushed into the market, past the stacks of cookies, pies, and bread – no Mario. Then around to the poultry shop with piles of chicken wings and blue cheese sauce in tiny plastic cups. He wasn't there. Then to the deli and cheese counter. Nope.

"Let's go to the back of the market," I suggested, even though Mario never frequented the wine or furniture stores. No luck.

"Where is he? What if he had a heart attack?" What if he was dead? Memories of Daddy flooded my brain.

Sienna started dialing her cell phone. "I'm calling Chester County Hospital." I wondered how she knew to do that.

We walked toward the car as she talked on the phone, but I couldn't hear anything with the noise of the passing vehicles. Once we got in the Jeep, she looked over and said, "He's there." I started to cry happy tears. He was alive.

She handed me the phone and drove out of the parking lot. The woman speaking introduced herself as the ER nurse in charge of Mario. "I want to warn you," she said, "he's had a *massive* stroke." The words had no meaning to me. I was just glad he was breathing.

Fifteen minutes later, we parked in the emergency room parking lot and ran inside. I asked for Mario, informing them I was his fiancée. After several urgent requests to see him, they walked us back.

He was in the far-left corner of the ward and attached to a forest of beeping machines and wires. Nurses and doctors were milling around. The left side of his face had drooped, and his right hand was jerking wildly. There was a pounding in my head.

He saw me and tried to talk, "My Dahma. My Dahma."

I ran over to his left side, which had fewer machines and wires, but the nurse motioned me to the right. "He won't be able to see or feel you on his left." My legs wobbled as I walked around the bed.

Looking for Sienna, I saw her talking to a man in a white coat at the nearby nurses' station. I took a steadying breath and kissed Mario on his forehead. His right hand found my waist and started moving wildly up my back. It took me a second to realize that he wasn't trying to feel me up. He couldn't control it.

"I'm ssssorry we're meeting like this again, my Dahma. I'm so sssssssorry," his tongue seemed thick and swollen.

Damnit! Why had I said that? "Don't worry 'bout that, baby. I just want you to be okay."

Sienna ran over with Mario's phone. "Mom, we need his passcode to contact his family to approve care."

"I cahn do ith," Mario insisted and reached for the phone with his right hand. Worried he might drop it, I held it steady while he entered the numbers. It took three tries, but he finally entered the code. Sienna rushed away.

Doctors and nurses kept pushing me aside to care for him. They needed to fly him by helicopter to University of Pennsylvania Hospital in Philadelphia. Unable to reach the family, they asked Mario to sign over care temporarily to me. He jaggedly signed a piece of paper on a brown clipboard. It looked just like the one Daddy used to hold his sermons. I bit my lip hard to keep from crying.

A nurse said they had to sedate Mario for the short helicopter flight because he was jerking around so much. She asked that we bring his prescriptions to the hospital since I couldn't remember all their names. I looked away as they shot sedation into his IV bag. Then watched them wrap him in a heavy red blanket. We nervously laughed when someone said he looked like an Italian burrito.

A tall, muscular thirty-something helicopter nurse introduced himself and asked for my number so he could text me when they arrived at the hospital.

"Don't ya be texthing my girlfriend," Mario said, surprisingly cognizant despite the sedatives. We all laughed.

"No love, you're the only man I want texting me."

A few minutes later, they presented him to me to say goodbye. The drugs had worked. His eyes were closed, his body still. I kissed him on the lips – and for the first time since our first date at The Gables - he didn't respond. I stepped back and the nurses handed me a plastic bag with his phone, wallet, and keys along with a paper bag with his clothes. I looked inside and saw blood on his shirt.

Sienna stood next to me as they rolled him through the double exit doors toward the helipad elevator. She grabbed my hand and led me through the emergency room exit door. We heard the helicopter's propellers roar as it lifted off. I stopped in the middle of the parking lot to see, but it was too late.

He disappeared into the clouds.

*

All I remember about the next two hours were the phone calls.

"Is this Donna?"

"Yes."

"We need your approval to do the following..." Then the nurse would describe the procedure they wanted to do. The percentage of success. What would happen if they didn't. The worst-case if they did.

"Do we have your permission to proceed?"

This happened several times. I can't remember what they asked, but the downside consequences dramatically worsened.

When we arrived at the house to pick up his prescriptions, the helicopter nurse texted me that Mario had made it to the hospital emergency room. He was alive and talking to everyone. I thanked him – and silently thanked the universe as well.

A few minutes later, a nurse from the neurosurgical department called to go over his medications. They couldn't wait until I got there with them. He had to go into surgery now. I slowly spelled out the names of the ten or so prescriptions. I asked the nurse how long the surgery would take. She said several hours, and hung up.

We took the dogs out, drove next door to retrieve Mario's car from the Amish Market, and threw his grocery bags in the fridge. I put together a canvas book bag with my knitting (Sienna had just taught me) and several books, including *The Untethered Soul*. As we left the house, I ran back to grab Mario's phone from the plastic bag.

I knew he'd want it when he woke up.

*

It was sleeting an hour later when Sienna drove us into the hospital parking garage. We rushed through the maze of ramps and winding halls until we found the neurosurgical wing. The nurses directed us to the waiting room. Some of Mario's family members were already there.

"He's still in surgery," his brother Tony said as he hugged me. Tony, a construction foreman like his father, was Mario's older brother. "I can't believe this is happening."

His wife, Marilyn, a small kind woman with a pageboy haircut and thick brown-rimmed glasses, stood quietly nearby. She came over to hug me and Sienna. Then I noticed her sister, niece, and Mario's younger brother. We all sat down.

Marilyn's first question surprised me. "You're engaged?"

I bent over in my seat to hide my face. I knew that Mario hadn't told his kids we were engaged because the boys were still against it. But I had no idea his siblings didn't know.

"We weren't making a big deal out of it. We aren't getting married until Sylvie graduates from high school."

They nodded politely, but I saw a couple of them look questioningly at each other.

Tony filled in the gaps, "The nurse said someone told Mario that his wife was on the way. He told them you were his fiancée."

"So glad he was talking," I said, trying to change the subject.

"That's a good sign," someone said.

"At least he wasn't driving when he had the stroke."

"It's good he wasn't with the kids."

"Glad he's at this hospital and not that one in Delaware." It was hospital small-talk full of fear, false assurances, and distraction. They were experienced at it – both of their parents had died within the last three years.

Eventually we ran out of things to say.

*

As we waited, some of Mario's family went for lunch. Sienna and I watched *Good Bones* in the waiting room. Not long after we were all together again, an older balding man with glasses, white lab coat, and pocket pens asked for Mario's family. Tony raised his hand. They were in charge now. I was relieved.

"The next twenty-four hours is key," the doctor said. "He made it through this first surgery, but if he doesn't regain consciousness and his brain continues to swell, we may have to cut away a piece of his skull. So the brain has room to expand."

I was glad to be sitting down.

"Remove his skull? That seems extreme. What if we don't?" Tony asked.

"He will die," the doctor said.

No one spoke. I started to weep. Sienna put her arm around me. I wanted the arm to be Mario's.

"They're getting him settled. Once he's ready, they will come get you."

I think someone thanked him, but know it wasn't me. I was unable to say anything.

*

After an hour, a nurse came to take us to Mario. On the way we walked past several rooms – one had an older man asleep with his head cocked sideways. One had a family in scrubs and booties. Finally, we saw him. He was propped up, eyes closed, his head half-shaved. In his mouth was a breathing tube and large beeping machines formed a fence around the bed. As I moved closer, I could see the beginning of angry stitches on the left side of his head. He would hate for anyone to see him looking this way.

The nurse smiled strength at us. "If you want to hold his hand, use the right one – he will feel it on that side."

I pulled a chair over and sat next to him. I gently took his hand. It was warm. I told him I was here. That I loved him. That everything would be okay. Even though he didn't respond or move.

Sienna found the remote and put the TV on mute with closed captioning. HGTV again. I moved away so the family could hold his right hand.

I picked up my knitting. The pink and white yarn picked weeks ago looked too happy for this place.

*

It was surprising how quickly the time passed. At dinnertime, the family left. They had a long trip home and there was nothing more to be done. No new decisions to be made. We just had to wait to see if he woke up.

I distracted myself with reading *The Untethered Soul*. It said our thoughts are not reality. They are only stories we tell ourselves to feel safe. My thoughts were no protection today.

Sienna and I stayed until the night nurse came on duty around 8 p.m. Then we left the hospital for home to take out the dogs.

Once there, we opened the fridge and looked in the bags of food Mario had bought that morning. Chicken wings. Chicken salad. The bread I loved. We had enough to last a week.

It was like he knew we'd need it.

*

Sienna and I drank a bottle of wine and ate the wings. Yogi, who loved Sienna more than all of us combined, slept at her feet. Jake crawled on top of me like the weighted anxiety blanket he'd become.

Tony texted to let me know Mario's kids knew about their dad. But they weren't going to bring them in because it would be too scary. I felt terrible that I hadn't even thought of how it might affect Sienna to be with me at the hospital. I just needed her. And I hadn't even told Sylvie yet because she was at Jim's.

Before passing out, I called the hospital. They immediately put me on hold and a cloying rendition of "Greensleeves" came on. It reminded me of the TV show *Lassie*, which used the song as its theme. After several choruses, Mario's nurse picked up. We'd talked hours before, but I had to remind her of my relationship to him. She said she couldn't give me any information. I wasn't family.

When I started to weep, she quickly said, "He's still asleep."

I thanked her and hung up. I told Sienna what happened.

"You've got to get Mario's family to tell them who you are. To put your name on the chart so they know to give you information."

*But I'm no one to him.* I drank the rest of my glass of wine and said, "I will. Tomorrow."

I don't know how I got into bed or when Sienna crawled in beside me. I do remember instinctively looking for a text from Mario. Then remembering, read through my frantic texts from that morning.

I wondered if he'd ever read them.

*Chapter Twenty-Five*

# FEEDING TUBES

On the road to Philadelphia and the hospital the following day, we saw people on the street dressed in Eagles jerseys and t-shirts. We'd forgotten. It's Super Bowl Sunday, and the Eagles were playing. Had it only been yesterday that Mario went to get wings?

When we asked, the nurse at the neuro ward desk said Mario wasn't responding. I could see Sienna's eyes widen, and I took her hand. Together we walked into his room and, when we saw him, froze. Mario's head had swollen so much overnight that he looked like a balloon person. I saw the attending nurse wipe a tear from her face as she typed notes into her computer. A chill flowed down my spine. Nurses saw everything. I sat next to Mario and held his right hand. Sienna pulled out her knitting.

Soon the family arrived, and about a half-hour later a team of doctors followed. They looked like a whitecoat posse complete with pocket pens, stethoscopes, and rolling computer desks. The lead doctor was tall and balding and had rimless reading glasses pushed onto his forehead. He turned his computer around to show an MRI of Mario's brain. My mind was spinning like a dime slot machine, so I couldn't make out what he said. But I did hear the words "massive stroke," over and over.

The team recommended removing a piece of Mario's skull. My left hand tightened gently around Mario's, and my right clenched the chair. I sat silently as the family discussed the situation. Someone worried the procedure would prolong his suffering. Another said it was the only way he would live. Don't forget his young children, a third reminded. They loved him so much and wanted to do the right thing.

I sat silently, listening to this debate over Mario's future. I both wanted a say – and didn't.

*

A few hours later, the lead nurse came back and encouraged the family to make a decision. I held Mario's hand as they finished their deliberations. And was relieved when they said to go ahead with the surgery. Within minutes, Mario's nurse came in to prep him.

We went to the waiting room, which held a new group of shocked and crying strangers. Sienna quickly suggested looking for the hospital's chapel. She had seen a sign for it on our way in. We set off down the twisting halls to find the sanctuary and discovered a semi-circular haven with pie sections, each with an altar to a different faith. There was even one with a large smiling Buddha and the Metta prayer posted beneath: *May you be happy, may you be safe, may you be healthy, may you live a life of ease.*

As Sienna knelt in front of a large picture of Jesus, I tried to meditate next to her, but couldn't. My mind whirred like a wind tunnel. I looked up at the Jesus picture, closed my eyes, and prayed silently, "Lord, I've been through so much – abuse, betrayal, death - and now my love is fighting to live. I don't deserve another heartache.

Please bring Mario back to me." I started to weep softly.

I looked over at Sienna and saw a cross on the altar near her head. It reminded me of my Father. My mind pleaded, "Daddy, please. *Please* let Mario come back to me. Please!" I waited for some kind of sign, but the room remained quiet. Eventually I quieted too.

After Sienna finished her prayers, we returned to the waiting room. We nodded hello to the family and took chairs on the side of the room. I pulled out *The Untethered Soul* and read from Chapter 14. It suggested letting go of what was happening and allowing "the peace that passes all understanding" to wash over me. Tears welled in my eyes. That phrase had been part of every service my father led.

It was the sign I'd been looking for. Daddy *did* hear me in the chapel. There would be no happy ending. No easy escape.

And whatever came, I would need the peace that passes all understanding to get through it.

*

An hour and a half after they'd prepped Mario for surgery, the doctor came in to tell us he had done well, but they couldn't confirm any real recovery for three days. Three days. Jesus rose from the dead in that time. I hoped Mario would do the same.

The family began gathering their things to go home. They were worried about football traffic and rioting Super Bowl fans if the Eagles lost. Reasonable, as they had always done so before.

After hugging them goodbye, Sienna and I sat in the now empty waiting room watching the game. At the end of the second quarter, a nurse came to say we could see Mario. When we did, I let out a huge exhale. He looked like Mario again. The swelling in his face was gone. Even his salt and pepper mustache and beard were intact. The only evidence of the surgery was a big white bandage where the left side of his skull had been.

I kissed him on the cheek, then sat and held his right hand. I was relieved it was warm. Sienna pulled a chair next to mine and grabbed my other hand.

When the attending nurse came in to check Mario's vital signs, she suggested we go home. She said any possibility that he would die was gone, and the anesthesia from the operation would let him sleep through the night. I kissed Mario's forehead and told him I'd be back in the morning. Sienna touched his shoulder and said she was sorry she had to go back to school the next day. She grabbed a tissue as we left the room.

An hour later, at home, we turned on the game. Seven minutes left. We hoovered the leftover wings and watched as the Eagles beat the Patriots to win their first Super Bowl. We toasted their triumph with the last of the wine.

We didn't feel guilty celebrating. If the Eagles could win the Super Bowl, anything was possible.

*

The following day, I dressed, woke Sienna, and asked her to take out the dogs while I went to the office. Before leaving, I packed a box full of macaroni and cheese, soups, and other food for her to take to college. She planned to leave around noon.

I put the box in her car and headed to the office to get my computer. I'd already emailed my boss asking if it was okay to work from the hospital, but was in too much of a hurry to wait for a reply.

After parking, I ran into her in the garage. I am twice her size yet fell into her arms, crying. Before I could speak, she said, "Of course you can work from the hospital."

Thanking her, I added that Mario still hadn't woken up. "I don't think we'll ever be married now," I sobbed. She kindly tried to console me.

I pretended that was possible.

\*

Sienna texted that she'd decided to stay one more day. I teared up in relief. When I got home, she was sitting with the dogs. Yogi was curled by her feet, Jake on her lap. We loaded our knitting, books, and computer bag in the Jeep and headed back to Philly.

When we got to Mario's room, the nurse was with him. "Mario? Mario?" she said. And then she pulled up an eyelid to shine a light in. His right eye and mouth twitched in response. We hadn't seen him move in two days, so we clapped.

"Is that good?" I asked.

"Yes. We're getting some movement on the right side. Not a lot, but some. Sit there and let's see if he'll squeeze your hand."

"Mario? Mario? It's me. Squeeze your right hand," I said. He squeezed my hand hard. "He did it! He did it!" He was still in there. Sienna hugged me.

The nurse poked his right foot. It shifted a little. No movement on the left side though, despite her insistent prodding.

When his family came, they were excited about his progress. The doctors arrived and were encouraged by his right-side movement, but said it was unlikely there would ever be any on his left. And again, they would know more in three days.

There was discussion of a feeding tube. The family asked to be consulted before one was put in. Someone said once it went in, it couldn't come out.

That didn't make sense to me. When I was alone, I asked one

of his nurses, "Can you take the feeding tube out once it's put in?"

All signs of emotion left her face. "It can be taken out if the patient can eat on their own."

I felt better and thanked her.

One of Mario's siblings called a few moments later to check on him. After I gave them an update, I said, "The nurse said they can take the feeding tube out – it isn't permanent."

"It's permanent if it's the only way he can survive."

It took me a moment to get it. And then I felt like Alice falling into an all new wonderland of dread.

*

I emailed Jim and asked if he could keep Sylvie for the next few days. Within minutes he wrote back, "I'm so sorry. Absolutely." His kindness was a brief respite from my despair.

I called Sylvie. She picked up. She never picks up.

"Mom? How's Mario?"

"He's doing okay, Lovie. But he's very sick."

"Is he going to die?"

I swallowed, "I don't think so, but I want to be here with him for the next few days. So, you're going to stay at your father's."

"Okay. Tell Mario I hope he gets better soon. Love you, Mom."

"Love you, too." I handed the phone to Sienna. She walked into the hall.

I squeezed Mario's right hand and looked down at the engagement ring he'd given me. His hand didn't respond this time. "That was Sylvie, Mario. She says she hopes you get better soon." No response. I watched the ring's five stones blur.

*

When the night nurse came on duty, I gave her an update on

Mario's responses – when he squeezed my hand, moved his right foot, or any sounds he made. Then we gathered our things to leave. After consulting the computer chart the nurse began poking and prodding. "Mario? Mario?"

I could hear a nurse a few doors down doing the same to another patient. And as we walked the empty black and white squares of the ward, we heard the echoes of patient names – as the nurses registered progress – if there was any.

*Chapter Twenty-Six*

# THE DEATH RATTLE

The following day, I sat with *The Untethered Soul* in one hand and Mario's hand in the other. Sienna had gone back to school and the family hadn't arrived. We were finally alone. Us and the bleeping machines. Their whirling swooshing sounds annoyed me almost as much as the hospital's hold music.

It was overwhelming – Mario's health, my medical phobia, our uncertain future. But I was facing it all. Had meditation and yoga sparked this sudden bravery? Or was it love for Mario?

Occasionally a nurse would interrupt to ask about movement in his hand. Most of the time the answer was no. I swiped through my Facebook feed and saw a meme that said, "Sometimes all you can do for someone is love them." That simple advice became my mantra.

I turned back to the book passage I was trying to read. It said we gain nothing from unhappiness. It only makes us suffer. There is always something that will make us unhappy; why let it?

Another nurse came in, and I watched Mario struggle to wake and comply with her commands to give a "thumbs up" or move his right foot. How could anyone be *happy* watching this?

I went back to the book. It suggested that when we decide to be happy, we will be faced with obstacles - and they will lead us to enlightenment. I took a big breath and let that thought wash over me. Was Mario's stroke a challenge along the freeway to spiritual growth?

If so, we needed an exit ramp.

*

Each day as we waited for Mario's resurrection, his brother Tony and I sat in his room. Other family members came and went, but most of the time it was Tony and me. While I answered emails, he worked on hidden word puzzles. Although we never talked about it, I was comforted that we had them in common.

Each night when the workday was over, I would go to the cafeteria and read *The Untethered Soul* over dinner. After, I would come back to the room and watch HGTV on mute with closed captioning until the night nurse came – making sure never to miss a reveal. Every happy remodel felt like a gift, a possibility.

Sometimes I would try to talk to Mario, but I felt uneasy when he didn't talk back. His uncharacteristic silence felt like he was already departed.

On the third day, I rolled my twenty-inch suitcase into the hospital. It carried my work computer, some framed pictures of Mario and the kids, and an old boom box. I hoped listening to his favorite classic rock station would give him comfort.

A family member called on the way in to ask about rehab hospitals for Mario near my house. Despite no significant change in his response, I was hopeful.

When I entered Mario's room, Tony was sitting on a comfortable grey pleather chair. He had on drug store reading glasses and was hunched over his puzzle book. When he saw me he stood, and we faced each other as if in a rugby scrum to discuss Mario's progress. After a few minutes, we broke the huddle to walk to Mario. I kissed him on the forehead and took his hand. I squeezed it but he didn't squeeze back. My upper body tensed and I let out a long exhale.

Opening my work laptop, I was soon sucked into an email chain. After I hit send on a problematic email, a tall thin young man entered the room. He had black-rimmed glasses, short brown hair, and a white coat.

After pleasantries, he said they needed to put a feeding tube in because Mario was having trouble getting enough nourishment. He said he also needed a tracheotomy and a ventilator because his body wasn't strong enough to handle his sleep apnea on its own.

He finished with, "It will make him more comfortable because he's spitting up blood from the tubes rubbing on the back of his throat." The words made me wince.

Tony stood up. "The family is going to need to talk about this first."

I put my computer aside and stood up too. "What're you really saying?"

"Yeah. Tell us the truth," Tony said. "We need to know."

Most times when the doctors discussed Mario's progress, they took the family into the hall. But this time, the doctor motioned for us to sit down. Then he stood facing Mario. "He will survive. The surgery that opened his skull determined that." He paused and went on, "But percentages say, he will not be able to walk again."

"But I read stories of…"

"Yes, there are miracles. But odds are, with this type of stroke, he will never speak, never walk without help, never be able to go to the bathroom. He will be bedridden for the rest of his life."

"But there are cases where the patient experiences a full recovery, right?" I persisted.

"Yes. But most of the time the patient never recovers more than he is now."

I looked over at Mario and it seemed like his body had slumped.

"Let me tell you a story," the doctor continued. "My grandmother had a stroke like Mario's. And even though I'm a neurosurgeon, my family was divided on what to do. They fought over her care, and despite my recommendation to put her in hospice, they insisted she go to a rehab center. She never recovered and lived in a vegetative state for three years."

My eyes blurred with tears. "He would hate that."

Tony went to Mario's side and held his left hand. "He would. He couldn't stand to see Mom when she was like that."

The doctor continued, "And there is no way for us to repair the damage that caused the stroke, so he will probably have more strokes."

I wept quietly. Tony turned away. The doctor didn't try to comfort us. He just stood there, firm and resolute. "I hope this story helps."

I looked up at him. "It does." We both thanked him, and Tony shook his hand as he left the room.

The song "Magic Carpet Ride" came on the radio. I sat down next to Mario and tried to take his right hand, but he somehow pulled it away and rested it on the bed rail.

"He used to do that out the car window when we were kids," Tony said.

I knew I should say something, but couldn't form words. I was a duck on water, calm on the surface, paddling like crazy inside.

"I'm going to talk to the family. He wouldn't want to live like that," Tony said, his voice cracking a little.

I nodded.

"I have to go," he said, rushing out.

In that moment, the sound of the machines became a comfort.

*

Ten minutes later, Tony came back with a priest in tow.

"Can you believe it? I ran into Father on my way out."

The priest was tall and looked around seventy. His grey-specked hair and horn-rimmed glasses reminded me of my father. He even had the same portable communion set.

He asked questions about Mario's case. We told him the doctor's grandmother story. "I walk these halls and see everything," he said. "And based on what you've told me, I think he's done."

"What do you mean?" I asked.

"Look at him." And we did. Mario was scrunched down and still. The nurse came to perform the hourly poking and prodding routine. When he didn't respond, she pulled up his right eyelid and flashed a light. He moaned and moved a little on the right side. It was like watching a baby being startled awake. But you would never do that to a baby.

"He's had enough of this," the priest said. "It's okay to let him go. It's the merciful thing to do."

Was a priest telling us it was okay to let Mario die? We watched speechless as the nurse recorded Mario's responses. She left the room.

The priest spoke, breaking our silence, "Do you want me to give him last rites?"

Tony choked out, "Yes."

The priest looked over at me, "Are you Catholic?"

"No, sir."

"Then I won't be able to give you communion."

"That's okay. I understand." I wasn't allowed to drink from Daddy's little cups either.

The priest was efficient. He was used to performing this sacrament quickly, mercifully. Within minutes the rite was over. Tony and I were alone with Mario. And the machines.

"Okay. I'm really going home now. We'll be back in the morning to talk to the doctors."

I nodded. And he was gone. I looked up at the clock. 7:45 p.m. The night nurse would be there soon. I packed up my knitting and computer and wondered when Mario would be relieved of this ordeal.

And how I would survive.

*

Mario's brothers and sister were already at the hospital when I arrived the following day. The decision had been made. They were taking him off life support.

I nodded – and kept silent. But my head was buzzing. I was grateful for Mario's family, who loved him enough to do what was required. But was also worried about what was coming - and sad, because we should have made it better.

The way he always had for us.

When the doctors and interns came with their rolling desks, the family stood. Someone said, "We've decided to withdraw care."

The head doctor stopped what he was doing, took off his reading glasses, and scanned the room slowly, making eye contact with every one of us. "This is the most humane thing you can do."

Several of us started to weep.

He continued, "I want you to know that everyone on this floor would want this decision made for us if we were in his condition. It's brave and loving of you."

The whirring in my head stopped. The doctor went on to describe the procedure of taking the tubes and machines away. The family said they wanted Mario transferred to the hospice center in Delaware, where his parents had passed.

I sat quietly mulling over what the doctor had said. We were doing the humane thing. What all the staff would have wanted for themselves. But if it hadn't been for the grandmother story, the priest's advice, and the family's experience, we might have done something inhumane. It felt so tenuous.

Like we'd passed a test we didn't even know we were taking.

*

We left while the nurses tended to Mario. When I walked back into Mario's room, the tubes and wires surrounding him were gone. The nurses had covered his head with a cap like a newborn, but his hair was still long on one side and he had a surgery buzz cut on the other. His breath sounded thick with mucus, and the inhales and exhales were lengthier than before.

"We've turned up the medication so he will be more comfortable," the nurse said.

I hadn't noticed her – the shock of seeing and hearing Mario this way had blinded me to all else.

It was then that I saw Mario's brothers and sister sitting to his right and his sister-in-law standing nearby. She motioned for me to sit next to him. I moved a chair closer and picked up his right hand, realizing for the first time there was no diagnostic reason to do so.

We could just hold hands.

*

Before going to the cafeteria for dinner, the family told me that Diana and the kids were coming soon.

I went out to the nurse's station to ask if they had scissors so I could cut his hair. The nurse looked through her drawer and handed me a pair. She followed me back into the room with a bowl that reminded me of the ones used to bathe babies. I took off his cap and started cutting his curls. The hairs fell into my hands, and I didn't want to throw them away, but felt awkward asking for something to hold them. I slipped some in my purse, then put the cap back on his head.

The nurse washed around his face, neck, and arms. She followed up with a towel. When she finished, she said, "He looks a little better."

"Yes. But not up to his standards. He'd want to look his best for the kids." I drew a finger across his stubbly beard, remembering how it once gave me brush burns.

Before leaving that evening, I picked up *The Untethered Soul* and read Chapter 17 – Contemplating Death. The passage suggested that death is there to teach us. To remind us that life is short and not to be wasted.

I let that seep in. When Mother died, I thought I was so enlightened, so above it all. I ignored and numbed the pain. Muscled through as if nothing had happened. I couldn't do that this time. I needed to feel and learn from this loss. Mario deserved that.

Maybe I did too.

*

Early the next morning I saw a text from Mario's sister. They moved him to the hospice center after midnight and she'd stayed with him all night. Tony was coming soon to be with him so she could go home. I got Sylvie off to school and headed down to the hospice center, carrying the boom box, family pictures, and my work computer. The hospice liaison said he could live for weeks. Even though Mother had died after only one night in hospice, I thought we had time.

I even stopped at Wawa for coffee.

At the center, I asked the front desk clerk for Mario's room and proceeded down a hall that looked more like a living room. There were couches and comfy chairs everywhere. As I drew closer to his room, I could hear raspy breathing – Mario. I turned to Tony and asked if he'd called the nurse.

He barked, "Of course we did. There's nothing we can do. They've done all they can." His energy propelled me from the room. I curled up in one of the rose-colored wingback chairs outside.

A few minutes later, Tony left and I went back in. I sat next to Mario and picked up his hand. He continued to breathe in a raspy way. "It's the death rattle," a niece said. "I remember the sound when Pop Pop died. He doesn't have much time."

She was young. I couldn't believe her.

I held Mario's hand in one hand while working on the computer with the other. His aunts and family members came in. Soon the room filled with noise as they talked about past hospice experiences and other family memories. One aunt was silent. She hugged me and sat in a nearby chair. The last time we'd been together was the funeral for Mario's mom (her sister). Her quiet presence comforted me.

Soon Tony came back with a couple of men I'd never seen before. He told me they were there to speak in tongues over Mario's body. Since Mario was not religious, I wasn't sure he would approve.

Even though the rest of the family left, I stayed.

While the men spoke, I held onto Mario's hand. But their words weren't words at all, more like sounds and syllables. I closed my eyes and saw colors behind my eyelids. Just like at the Reiki attunement. Red, green, yellow. As the men continued, the colors kept coming. It seemed to go on forever – and when they finished, I saw red, the root chakra color. I wondered what it meant.

After the men left, a woman with a beautiful toy collie came in. Still holding Mario's hand, I used the other to pet the dog and told her how we adopted Yogi and Jake. She asked what I did, and we spoke at length about yoga. For a few moments, I almost forgot why we were there.

As we talked, Mario's breath became less frequent. He was sleeping but had significant breaks between inhales and exhales. An older nurse with long grey hair came in with a clipboard and the dog and owner left.

The nurse said that since they hadn't gotten to know Mario, she wanted to ask some intake questions. To better care for him.

She asked about his kids.

"He always puts his kids first. He loves them so much."

The breathing kept stopping and starting. She asked what he loved to do.

"He loves history. He's a history teacher. And he enjoys cooking for his family – such a great cook. And he plays Pokémon Go any chance he gets."

She asked about my relation to him, and I told her I was his fiancée.

"Where did you meet?"

"It was such a romantic first date." I started to tell her about meeting at The Gables, how he had kissed me when we met, but before I could finish the story, Mario's breathing stopped. When it didn't resume, I grabbed the metal guardrail on his bed and turned toward the nurse, "Is this it?" Had I missed it?

She walked toward the door and yelled for another nurse. They went over to check Mario's pulse and waited. He took another quick inhale. And then silence. They checked his pulse and I watched them record the time of death in an ordinary tan file folder. I couldn't move. I touched his hand. It was still warm.

Maybe he heard me describe our first date as he passed. I hoped the memory was some comfort. I looked at his face. It was a shade lighter.

He was really gone.

It was impossible to believe, yet my body knew. It shuddered and gasped with the despair of all we'd lost. All that was taken. The happiness we deserved after years of doing the right thing. The dream of growing old together, in a bed and breakfast, bouncing grandbabies on our knees.

The reality of the loss hit hard. My mind pushed back hard. *No. No! Not again!!*

*

It doesn't matter how many times we lose someone, it always hurts. Our hearts always break. Because we loved them.

The only way out is through the pain - through the whole reality of what we've lost. We have to feel it, so we take nothing else in life for granted.

We must become more than what happens to us. Find joy wherever it's hidden. Be grateful for every thing, every moment, and every being.

Maybe this is what Mario and Daddy learned at all those death beds. Why they cared so much. Loved so well.

But I wasn't there yet. For me, this was another blow, another wound, another time left behind.

I folded over his bed and broke apart.

*

The family rushed into the room. They kissed Mario on the forehead, then cried and hugged each other. And me.

It took a while to recover, for the heaving to change to sobs, then slowly - a return to normal breathing. Eventually we wiped our noses, cheeks, and faces, and the family started discussing next steps. Where to have the funeral? Casket open or shut? I sat and listened. Unwilling to imagine any of it.

I didn't know what to do. Mario wasn't there anymore, yet I didn't want to leave him.

"Go home," his sister said. "You stayed with him to the end, Donna. There is nothing more you can do."

I nodded and kissed Mario on the head. Then started gathering my things. The boom box. The pictures. My work computer and cord. It felt weird doing all these everyday things, while Mario lay there not watching.

I hugged the family, left, and got behind the wheel of our seven-passenger SUV. I looked at the coffee cup – bought on the way down. When Mario was still alive.

I sent two texts. One to Michelle and one to Hope. Both said, "Mario is gone." I would wait to tell the kids when I got home.

As I drove along the same Delaware roads I'd driven with Mario, I sobbed. Billy Joel was right.

Only the good die young.

*Chapter Twenty-Seven*

# THE PEACE THAT PASSETH ALL UNDERSTANDING

As I readied the house for visitors, texts kept pinging from Mario's family with funeral arrangements. It would be Saturday, with an open casket.

"Can you pick out clothes for him?" his sister texted.

"Of course," I replied. "When do you need them?"

"Wednesday's fine. Don't forget shoes. Everyone forgets the shoes."

"I'll remember." I also remembered that Wednesday was Valentine's Day.

I thought back to a meme I'd posted for an *Elephant Journal* page before Mario's stroke. About a milk carton with a February 14 date on it. The caption read, "Even my milk carton has a date for Valentine's Day." Sienna had said, "Mom, you can't post a meme like that. You *have* a date for Valentine's Day."

Not anymore.

*

While drinking coffee the following morning, I took a picture from Mario's Facebook page, the one he used for his dating profile, and put my favorite Thomas Merton quote on it. "Love is our true destiny. We do not find the meaning of life by ourselves alone. We find it with another." It fit Mario perfectly. I added his name and the years of his birth and death along the bottom.

I posted it along with the link to his memorial service arrangements on both of our Facebook pages. Hundreds of people commented on the post.

*

Wednesday morning, I pulled up Mario's address in Google maps and headed the SUV toward his house. I'd never memorized the route because it changed depending on construction and beach traffic, and I always wanted to get there as fast as possible.

His sister texted, "Go ahead and take anything you want from the house."

When I entered his neighborhood, I started sniffling. And when I turned onto his street and saw the bushes we picked out, the broken driveway he'd never fix, and the doorway where he usually met me, I couldn't see the windshield anymore.

I unlocked the front door, and his smell embraced me. In the kitchen, I saw mail stacked on the table. On top was a large, padded envelope. Knowing he'd been buying gifts for Valentine's Day, I opened it. It was a small rectangular blue pillow – perfect for me to sleep with. It had white cursive writing that said, "It all began at The Gables. Donna and Mario." Below was the date we met. I held the pillow to my stomach and bent over. There was no sound at first, but then sobs took over my body.

For some reason it felt worse than the moment he died.

Eventually, calmed, I stood up, wiped my face with a paper towel, and placed the pillow on the table.

Climbing the stairway to the second floor, I looked in each of the kid's rooms. I noticed the perfectly sized dresser he'd found for his youngest son's narrow closet. And the pineapple bedposts painted yellow for his daughter's room. Finally, I stood in front of his oldest son's bedroom, admiring the black, white, and red comic-themed door. Only the most loving father would let his son put a full-size comic strip on his door.

In Mario's room, the bed was made, but clothes were strewn on top. The last place he'd gone was my house. He hurried too.

There was a glass next to his bed. He was the last person to touch it. I put it to my lips, pretending his were there.

In his closet, the scent of him intensified, reassuring and warming me. I wished it would never fade. Looking for the funeral outfit, I saw the yellow Polo sweater I bought that he never wore – it was too hot for him. And a grey plaid fleece shirt given to him last Christmas. I put that on.

There were no suits, but there was a blue sport coat. I pulled out a pair of tan khakis and laid them on the bed. Turning back, I pulled out a light blue striped tie he liked – and found a solid blue shirt with cuffs that needed cufflinks. He loved cufflinks – most bought on eBay. I found some in his side table and selected a pair of Italian flags he'd kept in a small square box.

I looked at the closet and paused as a wave of grief surged and went. Then searched in the bottom of the closet and found tan loafers. I put them on the bed. Next, matching dress socks and a pair of green and blue striped underwear. I wished I could see him strut around in them.

Turning back to the closet, I pulled out the maroon Henley long-sleeved t-shirt he let me borrow for gentle yoga classes. And the red plaid fleece shirt I bought him for our second Christmas. I also took the "You are my happy" accent pillow and grabbed the robes. Then cleared out my side table – placing the reading glasses and Yogi's water bowl in a bag.

It took several trips to drag everything down to the front door. I grabbed a wardrobe carrier from his basement closet and took the sport coat, shirt, and pants out to the SUV. I went back in and closed the door behind me. In the family room I saw the round glass art piece with a "family tree" in it that I'd given to him for our first Christmas together. I carried it to the craft closet to wrap it in newspaper, then walked it to the pile by the door. Turning back to the kitchen, I grabbed the blue pillow I'd found in the mail and the large red deep-frying pan he used for chicken marsala.

I wandered through the dining room to the living room and took down the hummingbird picture I gave him for his birthday. Everyone called him a hummingbird because he flew around doing everything for everybody. It was hard to believe that now he was still.

I stood looking at the pile of things. His things.

His sister-in-law texted me. "Do you have any Scripture recommendations for the funeral service?"

"Thank you for asking. I will send some tonight."

I made a few more trips to the car and then locked the front door. I paused for a moment looking at the house key. Should I leave it inside?

I dropped it in my purse.

*

After leaving Mario's clothes at his sister's, I headed home. On the way I stopped in one of my favorite stores. It's a privately owned shop that started as a shabby chic furniture store, but expanded over time to more styles and wealthier clientele.

While I was still in the parking lot, his sister texted me, "Do you want to write the obituary?"

The phone screen went fuzzy as I texted, "I would be honored." We agreed I'd send something to her before the end of the day. I locked my car and headed toward the store.

As I walked through the glass door, the bells on the door handle jangled. Inside were little living room and bedroom vignettes. On a wall was a framed quote, "Out came the sun and dried up all the rain." I felt like that spider, getting knocked down again and again. I took the picture off the wall and held it like a lifeline.

I turned and spied a blue denim chair next to a four-poster bed. I have a thing for chairs, which is ironic because I never sit in them. Always too busy. Always multi-tasking.

I sat in it. The comfy padding hugged me as I rocked back and forth and swiveled around.

Looking up, I realized the woman behind the counter was the owner. She had sold me the sectional I "won" in our divorce. And many other items since. She also had a rule about not letting clients buy off the floor.

"Can I buy this?"

She shook her head. "That one has to be ordered."

I choked out, "Does it help that my fiancé died two days ago?"

"Oh, I'm so sorry." She came from behind the counter with a tissue box.

I kept going, "I read an article this morning that you should have a place to grieve. Maybe it can be this chair."

She looked at me. I had bought so many items off the floor

when I wasn't supposed to. Every time, we argued. Every time, she gave in. This time she said without hesitation:

"Of course. Let me see if I can deliver it tomorrow."

Then it hit me – I was a widow.

*

That evening I wrote and sent this to Mario's sister for his obituary:

"Mario inspired others and tirelessly supported all to be their best. Although he was a passionate fan of history, a gifted history teacher, and a lover of antiques, Mario embraced new technology. He enjoyed playing Pokemon Go and sending memes to his children and friends. Mario also enjoyed cooking and experimenting with recipes, such as Beef Wellington, for his children. His kind and loving presence will be missed by many."

His sister thanked me and asked if I could do the eulogy.

I hesitated. The eulogy she gave at her mother's funeral was exquisite and eloquent. Full of inspirational stories and love. I couldn't imagine being able to speak at Mario's funeral, much less do the same.

I told her no, confident she'd do it instead.

*

The morning of the funeral, Sylvie and I loaded into Mario's car. It had sat in my driveway for over two weeks, both comforting and depressing me. Now I was driving it to his final resting place so his family could take it. When I backed the car out of the driveway, I heard a thumping noise coming from one of the front tires. Sylvie and I got out to look at it. It didn't look flat, so we shrugged and got back in.

We turned the car toward the funeral home in Delaware.

Thumping all the way. Following me were Sienna and her friend Noel in her car, my sister Deb and her husband in another, and their daughter and her five-year-old son in the last. I was grateful to have them with me. *Why do we wait for funerals to be with those we love?*

When we arrived about forty-five minutes later, the church parking lot was mostly full. I looked at the clock; we only had fifteen minutes till the viewing began. I walked side by side with my daughters into the church. The rest followed. I hugged several of Mario's relatives, then introduced everyone. As I walked toward the sanctuary, I heard someone ask Deb how I was. I wondered what she said.

Walking over to where they displayed the prayer cards, I noticed they'd taken the meme I created and used it for the card. I pulled a few tissues from a nearby box, dabbed my eyes, and entered the sanctuary.

Once I'd settled my family in pews near Mario's relatives, I walked toward the casket. I heard someone say how good he looked. And he did look much better than expected, but he wasn't my Mario. His hair was slicked back and almost black, rather than salt and pepper grey. Also, his face was greyish, and his mustache and beard were trimmed too short.

I took out the two things I'd brought to lay in the casket: the St. Louis baseball cap he wore because it was his mother's favorite team, and a coaster from a bed and breakfast we went to in Lewes, Delaware. Where the dream of owning a bed and breakfast together began. That was getting buried today too.

I put my hand on his. The coldness surprised me. Conscious of everyone looking, I stepped away and a family member gestured for me to stand at the end of the receiving line. The funeral attendants opened the doors and crowds came in.

The line was a blur. There were his students. Their shattered faces. The stories of how Mario edited their college essays, gave them lunch money, told them to shape up. How he'd been the only one that cared.

There were his friends. Telling me I was the best thing that ever happened to him. That he was happy after so many years. Unaware that we were only steps from his ex-wife Diana's family – and she was waiting in a car outside with their oldest son until the casket was closed. While her boyfriend watched the other two at home, too young to attend.

There were my friends, many more than I'd expected, considering the distance. Every time I saw one, I hugged them, even though many were from work and we'd never touched before.

As the time for the funeral service drew near, they shut down the viewing line. Each family member had a moment with Mario before they closed the casket. By this time I didn't care who was watching. I walked over and kissed Mario's cold forehead and touched his hand. I walked to the pew with Sylvie and Sienna and watched as the officiants turned the casket around, shutting my eyes as they closed it.

There was a hush as Diana and Mario's son walked down the aisle to sit with her family. Their two tall, slender figures hunched in unison. I remembered how much Mario liked to brag about his son's six-foot-four height. He looked shorter today.

There was no eulogy. I think his loss was too great, too shocking, too debilitating for everyone.

I wish I'd spoken - said what he meant to me.

How he found joy in simple things – an antique potato chip can, fresh mushrooms, ice cream from the local dairy.

And was generous to a fault – no one left his house empty-handed.

How he never lied. And bravely pointed out the truth his students – all of us – needed to hear.

How he accepted everyone – including embracing my children as his own. And knew what we needed rather than what we allowed.

How he taught me to love in a way that fundamentally changed everything. Before Mario, I looked down on giving without getting. After him, there was no other way to be.

How the hole he left will never be filled. Now I'll love and miss him.

Forever.

\*

I don't remember much else about the funeral. My friends told me the sermon was inspiring. That the kids were crying. That Sylvie put her arm around me. I can't tell you if any of that is true.

But during the benediction, I noticed the priest used the Scripture I'd suggested. The one my father used for his entire time in the ministry, from Philippians 4:7:

"May the peace that passeth all understanding, keep your hearts and minds in the body of Christ."

Mario had found his peace. Now I had to find mine.

# Chapter Twenty-Eight

# OUR TOWN

As the organist played the recessional, the pallbearers rolled the casket toward the exit. The priest motioned for Diana and her son to follow first, then my kids and me. The rest of the family fell in behind us. We paused at the back of the church while they lifted the casket into the hearse.

I could have ignored Diana. Everyone else did. But I sensed her sadness for her children and the man we loved.

Divorce makes us forget that we loved once. That for a time, our lives together were sweeter. Long after everything is signed, we may envision a time when we'll forgive - and are forgiven. For a wedding or after a grandchild.

But now? Letting any animosity persist felt reckless. Irresponsible.

I turned to Diana and said, "I'm so sorry for your loss."

She hugged me. "I'm sorry for yours. This just sucks."

I let out a quiet laugh. "Yes, it does."

The funeral staff secured the casket in the hearse, and since there was no graveside service, we headed to the country club for lunch. Inside the formal hall I found an empty table and sat down. My kids, Mitch, Deb and Ron, and Hope and Roy, sat with us. I felt the couples' empathy and fear. They had to think that this could, and would, happen to them.

I watched as Diana and her boyfriend tended to Mario's children's food likes and dislikes. Like it was a typical Saturday. The youngest two came over to greet us, one by one, and we gave them the small gifts my girls had purchased for them.

Later, after our table had walked the buffet and eaten, I went over to tell his sister how nice the casket looked. That Mario would have approved.

She handed me a package.

"Another Valentine's Day gift," she said. I had told her about the blue pillow.

I peeked inside. It was a black meditation bead necklace with a soft silk tassel. I had given him such a hard time about picking something for Valentine's Day, but it meant everything to get this now.

I thanked her and headed back to my seat. Quickly Googling the significance of the black mala beads, I found they were to be used while grieving. It was as if Mario had known I'd need them.

Placing the beads around my neck, I brushed the soft tassel on my cheek and watched as Sienna picked up Mario's youngest and Sylvie compared memes with his oldest. Until then I hadn't realized all they'd lost. Not only a father, but each other.

It was too much to bear. I quickly gathered my kids, said the expected goodbyes, and left his last family gathering – without him.

\*

That night, I woke to a black and white fluffy face. I could feel painful pressure in my forehead and tears rolling down my cheeks. Yogi was trying to lick them.

"Aw, thank you, Yogi," I scratched behind his ears. He turned his head to lick my hand. His tongue felt like warm sandpaper.

I tried to remember what I'd been dreaming but could only recall hearing Mother say, "The hardest time for me was after everyone left."

I wished I could ask Mother how she did it. How she survived when Daddy died. But she was dead too.

I pushed Yogi aside and unbuttoned Mario's fleece shirt. Underneath was my long sleeveless grey nightgown. Sienna jokingly called it my *Handmaid's Tale* outfit. I checked the time on my phone – 2:35 a.m. Rooting through the covers I found the blue pillow, then fingered the tassel of the black mala beads.

I scrolled through text exchanges with Mario. They reminded me of the play "Our Town" by Thornton Wilder. I had been in a local production of it right before I met Jim.

It's the tale of an ordinary town and ordinary couple. By its third act, we see the marriage and death of the lead, Emily, and her visit to town for one ordinary day. The narrator of the play says, "Choose the least important day in your life. It will be important enough."

Our time together passed like a three-act play. We met, we fell in love, and he died. And I had taken it all for granted. His love. The way he took care of us. That we had forever. Now, I would give up everything to be with him.

As Emily says, "Oh, earth, you're too wonderful for anybody to realize you."

*Chapter Twenty-Nine*

# ARE YOU UP TO THIS?

When the alarm went off, I popped out of bed, started the shower, and plugged in my hot rollers. It had been a couple weeks since the funeral and everyone but Sylvie was gone. And if I didn't hurry I'd be late for my therapist's call.

Within what seemed to be seconds, the phone rang. I turned off the shower, wrapped myself in a towel, and answered it.

After our usual pleasantries, Michelle asked, "Now, *how* are you doing?"

"Feeling sad and a little scared. Sylvie's going to her Dad's tonight."

"That must be tough."

"It's the first weekend I will be alone since Mario died." I took a Kleenex and wiped away some moisturizer and a tear.

"Okay. Remember to eat, sleep, and stay hydrated. It will be much worse if you are hungry or tired."

I took a sip of water. Then started putting on foundation.

"Are you working yet?"

I looked down at the orange and black mascara bottle. "I am. It helps to be busy. But I keep my office door closed and have been avoiding wearing mascara so they can't tell I've been crying."

"Oh, Donna."

"I just don't know how I'm going to live without him."

"One of my friends was married a long time and her husband suddenly died too. She said at first, it helped to think of things that would annoy her about him. That it helped not to idolize him so much."

"Well, there were things that bothered me." How guilty it made me feel to say that.

"Another thing that might be helpful is the idea that grief comes in waves. Sometimes it's very intense. And sometimes, you don't feel it at all."

I couldn't imagine *not* feeling Mario's loss, but thanked her for the advice.

"How are the kids doing with everything?"

I told her that initially Sylvie was devastated, but she was feeling better now. We were spending more time together. Walking the dogs and watching disaster films, which she likes as much as I do. But Sienna was having a difficult semester. She missed some mid-terms because of the funeral. I even had to send a copy of his obituary to the school so she could retake one exam. And she keeps having trouble with her stomach. "I think it's just nerves, but wish I was closer than five hours away."

Michelle suggested Sylvie and I take a trip to see Sienna in Pittsburgh. My heart leapt at the thought. When I finished the session and got into the office, I Googled "dog-friendly hotel" and found one near her university. I booked it for an open weekend when I'd have Sylvie.

\*

Hours later, my boss popped into my office and closed the door.

"Do you have a minute?"

I'd never said no to this question. She proceeded to ask me to take on two new reports and project management for the European Market.

Even though I had sidelined my day job in favor of a role that was better for my mental state, yoga had made me a better worker and manager. The result? More responsibility and visibility.

"I realize you've been through a lot recently. Are you up to this?"

"I think so. It might be good to have something new." I almost believed what I was saying.

"I don't know how you're doing it. The divorce, your mother, and now losing Mario."

"Don't really have a choice." My voice sounded annoyed, angry. She pulled back and I instantly regretted snapping back like that. She'd been so kind and caring, and the extra work would help fill the void in my life. "Sorry, just trying to accept it all and keep moving."

She looked closely at me. "Well, let me know if I can do anything."

"Thank you."

She nodded, thanked me, and opened the office door. She asked if I wanted it closed or open.

I could feel tears close by. "Closed."

*

Saturday morning I took a long walk in the neighborhood, making sure to wear black sunglasses. The shades felt like a barrier, so no one would stop me to talk, or see what felt like craziness in my eyes.

As I walked, birds kept stopping in front of me on the sidewalk or mailboxes. Birds I'd never bothered learning the names of before. I Googled them. Red-headed finch, tufted titmouse.

Birds too whose names I learned in elementary school. Robins, blue jays, and cardinals. Lots and lots of cardinals. Had they always been there? Or were they signs from Mario? He always said loved ones visited through cardinals.

And what were those red, green, and yellow colors I saw right before he passed? Was that his spirit?

Could Mario's energy still be here? Was he trying to reach me?

*

After sunset, I bundled up to meet my former yoga teacher and friend Mary, the one who recommended Yoga Rob's school. She was grieving too - her mother died days after Mario. As I entered the dark and noisy bar, I saw her at a table in the back. She had a glass of wine. She stood to hug me and we both sat down.

"How're you doing?" she asked.

"Okay. I'm halfway through my first weekend alone since he died. It's been awful, but not as dreadful as I'd expected."

"Anticipation can be worse than reality."

"Sometimes."

"Have you been here before?"

"Yeah, but not with Mario. I can't go anywhere I've been with him."

"I get that."

"Yup, and I also avoid places I used to go with my ex, so I might have to find a new town to eat in."

She grinned, "That's a lot of work."

"It is. Grief is exhausting."

"I know. No one understands."

"And sometimes I cry all the time, and sometimes not at all, and feel guilty when I don't."

She nodded and we shared grief stories. Both of our mothers

were "difficult." We were their black sheep. That could be why we connected in the first place. They call them trauma bonds.

We ordered one round, then another. Mary reminded me that Yoga Rob had warned us not to numb ourselves with alcohol.

Although we knew he was right, we toasted to him.

*

That night I woke with a song playing in my mind. The line that lingered was "I want to die in your arms." I propped myself up on one elbow and grabbed my phone. Google said it was "Annie's Song" by John Denver.

Two furry faces filled my view. I scratched behind Jake's ears as Yogi crawled next to my belly. "I don't know what I would do without you." I looked at my cell phone – 2:40 a.m.

I left them in the family room to get a glass of water. When I returned, Jake had taken my spot on the couch. I shoved him aside so I could lie down. He settled at my feet and Yogi curled at my chest. Drifting off, I wondered if the song was like the cardinals – a way for Mario to let me know he was still here.

*

The next day passed with an hour of elliptical, yoga class, a massage, and reading Mary Oliver poetry. She felt like a kindred spirit with her abusive childhood, lost love, and devotion to dogs.

After the massage I started writing an article about *The Untethered Soul* and how it helped me survive Mario's passing. Once I began, the words came quickly. By dinnertime I submitted the first draft to *Elephant Journal*.

After eating, I started reading through Mario's edits of my book at the kitchen bar. In his notes he suggested I include the title of a Sarah McLachlan song. I picked up my phone and searched on Pandora for her playlist. I hit play. The song "Fallen" came on immediately. I added the title to the book draft but didn't turn off the playlist.

I came to the passage about Mother and how after my dad died, the hardest thing for her was not to have him there to scratch her back. The realization that she had no one to be intimate with was devastating. When I read that paragraph, edited by my lost fiancé, while listening to Sarah McLachlan, I started to cry. For the loss of Mario, and my mother too.

The dogs rushed into the kitchen. Yogi barked at my feet and Jake jumped up and put his paws on my shoulders to hug me. I walked into his paws, then bent to scoop up Yogi. We went and cuddled on the family room couch. Jake brought a stuffed animal for a game of catch. Just like he'd done with Mario weeks before. He missed him too.

I tossed the toy with Jake until he lost interest and crawled onto my lap. Yogi nestled at my feet as I turned on the finale of *Master Chef*. It was one of Mario's favorite shows. I wondered if he already knew who won.

*

A few weeks later, alone in the family room, I swiped through emails on my phone. There was one from the dating site *Our Time* – the one I'd used to meet Patrick and Mario. My finger hovered over the "Join" button in the email. It was seven weeks since Mario's stroke, five since he died. What was I thinking?

I *wasn't* looking for a relationship or someone to replace Mario. That was impossible.

What I *was* looking for was male companionship. A friend. The chance to be someone other than the grieving widow. For conversations to start with something other than, "So how're you doing since Mario died?"

And in my defense, growth isn't linear. We are repeatedly given triggers – opportunities. Chances to lean into our fears. To test our awareness. To fail for a time.

I hit the link for the site. Like before, it immediately went through the steps of starting a dating page. Pushing down the fireworks in my chest, I loaded likes (which included someone who exercises and eats healthy) and dislikes (like bar hopping and hockey). Then I uploaded the picture I'd used before. When selecting status, I chose widow, although technically I wasn't. But maybe if I met others who'd lost loves, I could ask them how they got through it. How they lived with the emptiness.

I paused before hitting the link to make the page live. What would everyone think if they knew I was doing this? Mario's family probably wouldn't speak to me again. And what about my kids? Is this the kind of example I wanted to give them? I almost left the site right then. But last time it had taken months to get an in-person date.

I hit the "go live" link.

*

The following day, I woke up minutes before the alarm and scrolled through my emails – there were over twenty notifications from men on *Our Time*. I put the phone down. No time for this nonsense.

I put on leggings and my YMCA shirt and headed to the gym.

When I got to the Mind Body studio, I cued up a new playlist. Journey's "Don't Stop Believin'" came on. I smiled and laid a yoga mat in the front of the room, and told the students what props they would need.

Some asked how I was. I said I was "getting there," although I had no idea where *there* was.

When "Day Break" by Medwyn Goodall came on, I walked up and down the line of mats asking the students to be aware of their breath. To let go of what they came in with for the length of the class. To connect with their bodies and spirit for this short time.

And within minutes, the tears that were usually so close receded. I was home.

*

A few hours later, while I was looking at my phone at work, a text appeared.

"Hey. How are you?" Patrick. *Oh no! Had he seen my page on Our Time?* I paused for a few moments, then replied, "Not great. My fiancé died last month." I knew it was a bit blunt – but didn't care.

He texted back immediately. "Oh my, I'm so sorry. Can I do anything?" I could feel the pull of his gentle kindness through the phone.

But I wasn't in the mood for his sympathy. "No. Just need to get used to being without him."

I put down the phone and went back to work.

*

Later that day, Patrick texted, "I know it's short notice, but would you want to grab coffee?"

I didn't need a pity latte from the man who'd dumped me. "Sorry. Have my daughter tonight. Need to get home to make dinner."

*

The following morning, I woke to a text. At first, I thought it was from Mario. He'd sent me a song and birds, but he couldn't text, right?

209

"Good morning. Thought this might make you smile." Patrick. He sent a YouTube link to the Sting song, "Every Little Thing She Does Is Magic."

My heart warmed a smidge, like in *The Grinch*. He'd remembered my thing for Sting.

*

As the days passed, the messages from men on *Our Time* kept coming. Most candidates were too old or creepy, with one exception. His name was Dan, and he was over six feet tall, a father of three, and a computer project manager. I replied to his message. He responded a few hours later and we started messaging. Within a few days I knew he had a good sense of humor, liked to hike, and had a son going to the same college as Sienna.

At the same time, Patrick was texting me a song link every morning. It was hard getting out of bed to a world without Mario. But Patrick's texts helped. He probably felt sorry for me. Maybe we could be friends?

When he asked to meet for breakfast, I agreed.

Later that same day, Dan asked to have coffee the following weekend. My face warmed and red splotches appeared on my chest. I wondered if I'd mistakenly opened the universal male companionship floodgates. Unlike Patrick, who had put himself in the "friend zone," Dan was looking for a relationship.

Even though my body told me not to reply, I agreed to have coffee with him.

*

The following Wednesday, I parked outside DK's Diner. I'd picked DK's because I'd never been there with Mario.

When I walked into the restaurant exactly on time, Patrick

stood up from a table in the back. I walked over and we looked at each other. He was handsome in his button-down light blue shirt and jeans. I noticed a navy-blue sport coat on the back of his chair and opened my arms to hug him. When we pulled back, I saw his smile and the way the corners of his blue eyes crinkled.

After he shared condolences for Mario and asked how I was doing, we launched into light conversation. I caught him up on my kids and he did the same. I told him about adopting Yogi and Jake and he mentioned that his dog Samson had recently had cancer surgery. I watched his smile evaporate as he described how close he came to losing him.

We discussed our hobbies and I told him about my article and book writing. He told me about the latest book he'd published. He mentioned he'd kept a copy for me at the book signing I'd blown off in December. I tried to gloss over that by telling him about my recent *Elephant Journal* article, which received an Editor's Pick designation. But couldn't help feeling bad about missing his book event.

Patrick mentioned he was taking his family to Ireland for his birthday in October. It had always been his dream to go there. I told him about the upcoming yoga retreat in Mexico that I was helping to lead. The conversation was light and lively. I laughed a lot and felt both happy and guilty at the same time.

Time flew by, and soon we had to leave for work. He asked if we could get together when I returned from Mexico.

I said yes.

*

On Sunday morning I subbed for a gentle yoga class. Right after it ended, I noticed a text from Dan that he was at our preappointed Starbucks, wearing a red sweater. My yoga-induced calm vanished. I was late.

I texted back an apology and said I'd be there in fifteen minutes.

Twenty minutes later, sweaty and flustered, I walked into the coffee shop. A man matching Dan's *Our Time* picture stood up. He was tall and balding with long legs and an average middle-aged paunch that matched my own. After we ordered our coffees – mine a skinny latte, his black – we sat at one of the high-top tables. A few weather-related comments in, I asked, "Do you have any trips coming up?

"I am heading to the Adirondacks for a two-week backpacking trip in a couple months."

"Two weeks? Will you be alone?"

"No, I'll be with my three best friends. But I have backpacked alone for weeks before. Have you ever been camping?"

"Only with the Girl Scouts. And that was in cabins with running water."

"Would you ever want to go real camping? In tents?"

I slumped a little. I usually defined camping as hotels without room service. "Maybe. I could give it a try." I kicked myself for not saying how I really felt.

He smiled and I felt I'd passed an important test. But I couldn't help comparing the effortlessness of the first time I met Mario or the breakfast with Patrick to this.

As we finished our coffee, we discussed our jobs. We were both project managers and it felt good to connect on business stories, something I used to do with Jim. We compared favorite restaurants and mine, The Whip Tavern, was new to him.

He shared that he was only recently separated and missed

being in a relationship. It made me remember how sad I was after my separation. He said he wasn't having much luck on *Our Time*. When he asked about my online dating experience, I told him about finding Mario and his recent death.

Dan went silent.

*Okay, I'm off the hook. He can't want to go forward now.*

But he said he was sorry for my loss and gracefully changed the subject to the kind of music he liked, including Pink Floyd and Boston. I liked both bands, but preferred Patrick's list. Why was I constantly comparing?

Coffee finished, we started to glance at our phones. He asked what I was doing the following week. My left leg started bouncing on the lower rung of the coffee bar stool. I told him about the yoga retreat in Mexico and that I would be gone until the end of the month. He said he was going to Vermont the following week, and we laughed about going in entirely different directions. He asked if we could go out when he came back.

I said yes. Even though the thought made my stomach churn.

But maybe by then, I'd be ready.

# PART FOUR

## Shanti

"Each moment is an opportunity to make a fresh start."
*The Places That Scare You* by Pema Chodronn

*Chapter Thirty*

# SEAWEED

The last time I visited Mexico I arrived alone and had a fiancé at home. This time I flew in with my friend Samantha. And at home I was alone, because my fiancé was dead.

I had to keep saying the dead part because it didn't feel real.

As we walked out of the airport with our roller cases, I noticed all the men gawking at Samantha as she passed. Why wouldn't they? She was dressed in billowy blue pants and a cool crisp white cotton shirt. Her espadrilles had straps that crisscrossed up her delicate calves. With her long wavy blonde hair, she looked like Gwyneth Paltrow, only prettier. I had on pink flamingo flip-flops and a black and white sundress. I looked like a rom-com sidekick, only sweatier.

A few miles from the airport, the driver of the Maya Tulum van asked, "Beer?"

We looked at each other and nodded yes. He drove off the highway onto a mostly dirt road. When he parked at the small mini-mart, we noticed a couple men smoking by the left side of the building. They stopped and glared as we walked past. I realized no one knew where we were.

"Where's the beer?" I asked the tattooed man behind the counter, hoping "beer" was a universal language.

He waved me toward a beverage refrigerator and I picked a sixpack of Coronas, paid by credit card, and walked outside. Even though the glaring men had left, I sprinted to the van and locked the door once Samantha was inside. A few minutes later we were back on the highway. I looked at the passing trees and wondered if there'd been any reason to be fearful, or was I predisposed to tragedy now?

I opened a can of beer and handed it to Samantha, then opened one for myself. We hadn't talked much since I assisted her at last year's retreat, so we used the beer and two-hour ride to catch up. She did most of the talking. I was tired of my own story.

When she finished describing her recent break-up, I checked my phone. There was a text from Patrick. I curved the device away from Samantha's view.

"Did you make it to Mexico okay?"

*Aw, that was nice.* "Yes. Thank you for checking on me."

"How was the flight?"

"Uneventful. Even managed to write an article for *Elephant Journal*."

"If you want to send it, I'll take a look."

Mario used to do that. He always kept me from sharing too much. "That would be great. Thank you."

When we arrived at the resort, the receptionist handed us a fruity cocktail and took our registration information. We were in luck. Our cabana was ready.

The bellboy led us to a sand and stone pathway. On the way he pointed out the large restaurant to the left and the spa pathway to the right. When we arrived at our thatched hut, a small, sculptured foot bowl filled with water flanked the left side of the door. Someone had left two pink and peach blooms in it. One blossom was open, one tightly closed.

When we finished unpacking, I suggested we go to the beach. As we neared the ocean I commented on an unpleasant smell, and when we got to the sand, piles of brown and black gunk were strewn between it and the water. Pathways were still visible, but the smelly substance was everywhere. It was dotted with plastic milk bottles, soda cans, and other debris. The birds were picking at them.

"Dead seaweed," Samantha said. "This happened a few years ago too."

I was glad room and board were complimentary in exchange for working the retreat.

"Let's make spa appointments," I said. Samantha nodded and we headed toward the front of the resort.

"You should get a treatment with Sandra," Samantha said as we walked. "She's my favorite masseuse."

When we got to the spa reception area, a raised open deck with a roof, I asked the spa manager about Sandra's availability. He said she had an opening the following day and asked what kind of treatment I wanted. He pointed to her bio hanging on a wooden wall to our right.

Her description said she was a masseuse, Reiki Master, and EFT practitioner. I knew what the first two were but had no idea what EFT was.

"I just want a massage." I wasn't in the mood for anything new.

\*

The following morning, I left my flip-flops by the bed and walked barefoot to the spa. I checked in with the receptionist and poured some cucumber water into a small glass before sitting on an overstuffed chaise lounge next to the other patrons. Once the retreat started, I would know everyone around me. For now, I could be anyone.

A small thin woman with black glasses walked up. "Donna?" she asked in a foreign (but not local) accent. I nodded yes and shook her outstretched hand.

As we walked to her hut she asked, "Just a massage?"

"Yes. I've been through a lot recently and need to relax." She nodded. I wondered, as a Reiki master, if she could sense why I was *really* there. I missed being touched – and hoped the massage would release "the issues stored in my tissues."

Sometimes when I get massages, it's like I'm being pummeled to death. Or the practitioner spends so long in one area that I want to scream. But Sandra's touch was gentle, benign. It was like peace was flowing into me.

As we walked back to the reception desk, she stopped on the sandy path and said, "You are very sad."

I nodded. My face wrinkled and tears filled my eyes. "I just lost my fiancé. He died earlier this year."

She hugged me and handed over a tissue from her pocket. "You need to come back for my signature treatment."

I blew my nose into the tissue. "I think I do." She put her slight arm around me, and we walked to the receptionist.

*

The day of my second appointment with Sandra, I got up early and pattered up to the restaurant.

I took a table by the window even though the sky was dark. Opening my journal, I picked a Daily Zen Calendar quote page from the stack paperclipped to the cover. I used an app to "meme" it using a photo from the day before, then scheduled it to post a couple hours later when more people would be awake. I'd begun this practice the day I posted the meme about Mario's death. I intended to post one every day until the first anniversary of his passing. It gave me purpose. A way to honor him. Another reason to wake up.

I opened Pema Chodron's *The Places that Scare You.* The chapter for that day was on how we're always in transition. To expect things to stay the same creates suffering. And we know this. We know things are constantly changing, but we still rail against the shifts.

But how many changes can one endure in three years?

I put my mug on the bar, nodded at the growing number of restaurant workers, and walked toward the beach. The sky was grey and brown now and other retreaters were standing or walking on the sand, waiting for the sun to rise. I smiled hello but kept moving, dodging the expanding piles of seaweed as I went.

Rays of light broke through the sky, but still no sun. I looked at my phone to check the time and saw a text from Dan comprised mostly of emojis. Frowning, I texted him back with no emojis. It was the first text from him since I left. On the other hand, Patrick had been messaging me a song each morning and several more texts throughout each day. He'd even edited my second article about Mario - which *Elephant Journal* had immediately accepted.

I took a few pictures of a seagull flying into the headwind and watched as he playfully glided up and down despite the obstacle. My gaze drifted down the beach. Retreaters were heading to their rooms. Time to go.

When I arrived at the main yoga hall, no one was there. I put on meditation music and began laying yoga mats, blankets, and straight-back floor chairs in a circle. As students arrived, I greeted them with a nod - then stood by the door to let in those who were late. There were always a few.

After meditation ended, I helped everyone put away their props and then headed to breakfast. Last year I'd sat with the students like a good retreat assistant and engaged in conversation. This year it was too hard. It helped that yoga teachers are expected to be calm and quiet.

After breakfast I headed to the smaller hall to set up for yoga class. I pulled a mat out for Samantha and set it in the front of the room with a blanket and two blocks.

With minutes to spare I pulled out a mat for myself. As assistant, I rarely had time for my own practice, so this was a treat. Sun salutation, cat-cow, butterfly, tortoise, and finally child's pose. Even though it should have worked, I felt no peace.

Once class began, I walked around the room and adjusted postures to prevent injuries. Some students took the adjustments and appreciated the props I offered. Some resisted. I tried not to judge them.

As everyone settled into relaxation pose, Samantha and I went to each person and gently cradled their feet and heads in our hands. After class, one of the students asked if I did Reiki. Surprised I mentioned taking the first level training. She said to continue because she felt much clearer after my touch. I thanked her for telling me and wanted to ask more, but I was late for my treatment with Sandra.

Before I could pour a glass of cucumber spa water, she greeted me. We walked to her hut. Inside, I started to take off my clothes, but she stopped me, "For this treatment you stay clothed."

Hmm, was I going to get my money's worth? We stood next

to the massage bed. She looked almost frail except for the muscle definition in her biceps.

"Have you ever heard of EFT?" she asked.

"No."

She shared that after years of providing massage and Reiki treatments she saw her clients continue to suffer from pain and trauma in their bodies. She did some research and discovered EFT – Emotional Freedom Technique – and trained in it.

She showed me a piece of paper with markings on different areas of the human body. The area above the eyebrows, the outer crease of the eye and the spot below, the upper chest, the area below the armpits, and the point between the knuckles of the ring and pinkie finger.

"These are zones you tap with your fingertips. The tapping releases emotion and pain. Like acupuncture but without needles."

My forehead wrinkled and my mouth twitched sideways.

"Just try it."

I nodded and looked down at the paper she'd given me. It looked like a diagram from the kid's game "Operation." I hated that game.

She motioned for me to sit down on the massage bed. "Let's start with the trauma. Did you experience trauma with your fiancé's death?"

"What do you mean?"

"Were you there when it happened or during treatment?"

"Yes," I said quietly.

"That is trauma – and you're still reliving it, yes?" I nodded, my eyes filling. She handed me a tissue.

"To release it we need to experience it while tapping at points on our bodies. Each time we do this we rate the trauma feelings on a scale of one to ten. And keep tapping until the rating is close to zero."

I'd spent a lifetime avoiding pain. "This could take a while."

"It will if you resist. You must feel the feelings to release them. So much of grief is reaction and resistance to trauma." My body stiffened and my breath quickened. I looked toward the hut doorway. I didn't want to relive anything.

She gently pushed me back on the bed so my feet were dangling like a child's. She asked me questions about the day of Mario's stroke. The fear I felt when he wasn't back from the market. The moment I saw him in the hospital. Waiting for him to get out of surgery. Seeing him deteriorate. His last breath.

I started the process with a trauma rating of ten. After three rounds of crying and tapping it was at a four. I'd stopped crying, but that wasn't good enough.

"Do you have guilt?" she asked.

"No."

"Are you sure?" Her eyes glowed like bright interrogation lights.

I broke. "If I'd known he was going to have a stroke and die, I wouldn't have focused on the stupid stuff. Like freaking out over the kids or him playing Pokémon Go all the time. I would've listened to him more. I wouldn't have drunk the night before the stroke. I would've gone with him to the market that day…"

"All of these feelings are normal. You loved him, right?"

I nodded yes.

"He knew you loved him, yes?"

"Yes."

"Guilt is a wasted emotion. It does nothing to help. It only hurts. Let's tap away the guilt."

We went through the tapping process, and I re-rated my trauma feelings. Zero. I felt sweaty and exhausted, like I'd just finished a marathon.

"Okay. Now we work on the loss."

There was a roaring "No!" sound in my head. Out loud, tentatively, I said, "Okay."

"Let's talk about the loss. Do you miss him?"

"Yes. We were together as much as we could be living forty minutes apart. I miss him so much."

"And this makes you sad."

"Very sad."

"Can you think of happy times with him?"

"Well, yes." There were so many. When we cooked together. The Lewes weekend when we saw our first beach sunrise. Editing the book pages – resting now at the bottom of my suitcase.

"Try to connect to him through happy memories. You don't have to connect to him through sadness. You don't have to be sad to remember him. You can be happy thinking of him."

It took me a moment to let that register. "You're right." And maybe that's why Mario got so sick – he never got over all his losses.

Sandra motioned for me to continue.

"I need to find a way to do that," I said. "I read that if a widow stays in traumatic grief for more than six months, she can develop serious health issues twelve to fifteen months later."

"That's because they connect through sadness. They feel guilty if they don't connect that way."

"That makes sense."

"I'm from Sicily."

"Oh, wow, Mario was Italian. He would've been so happy I met you."

"Maybe, but I'm Sicilian – not the same."

I smiled remembering how important it was to Mario to differentiate exactly where his family was from, too. "Of course."

"In my country, they dress widows in black and make them stay alone in mourning 'til they die. But you don't have to follow Mario to the grave. You're young. You can live."

"I'm not sure I want to. I know it's unhealthy to think that way. But I doubt anyone will love me like Mario did."

"Maybe not. But there are different kinds of love, yes?"

I nodded but didn't say anything. Her words reminded me of Yoga Rob's advice after I found out about Jim. That we're supposed to be in multiple long-term relationships. To help us learn to love ourselves and others. And maybe after experiencing Mario's love, I can be a better partner for someone else. When I'm ready.

"What is your level of sadness now?" she asked.

I thought about it for a second. Then said, "An eight."

"So, think about a phrase that captures your feeling of sadness and a phrase that supports you. Something like: 'I'm lonely for Mario, but love and accept myself as I am.'" I squirmed. Sounded like something from a sappy self-love meme.

She noticed my reaction and said, "It's okay. Just try it while we do the tapping."

She guided me through the tapping procedure while saying the phrase each time. At the end she asked me to tap my hand while moving my eyes around in circles, up and down, then side to side. After, she had me hum a tune. I felt my body resist yet went along.

When we finished I took a long inhale and exhale. She asked, "What is your sadness level now?"

I smiled. "A two."

She took her glasses off and wiped her forehead with a towel. "Good. One more round of tapping and you're done."

After we finished the last tapping series, I closed my eyes. My body wasn't as heavy and I could breathe easier.

As we left the hut, I noticed red, yellow, and orange flowers flanking the sand walkway. They must have been there before, but I hadn't seen them.

When we arrived at the reception area, she gave me a piece of paper explaining EFT, the tapping procedure, and the website that explained how to get certified.

She smiled and gently wrapped her thin arms around me. I hadn't felt this peaceful since Mario left for the Amish Market.

"Share what you've learned."

I nodded and watched her scurry away.

*

Later, Samantha and I met in the restaurant for dinner. Fifty-ish yoga women "at ends," we had on makeup and going-out clothes. She was dressed in a short Lily Pulitzer long-sleeved dress, and I was in a maxi strappy dress with salmon pink, white, and grey flowers.

"Your energy is lighter," Samantha said.

I nodded. "You were right about Sandra."

"You had the tapping treatment?"

"Yup. She told me I had to experience the grief to get through it. That resisting was the problem. I feel like a new person." What if that is the key to everything? Going through the pain rather than around it.

"I need to get me some of that," she said with a laugh.

The waiter came and even though the place was known for healthy vegetarian fare, we ordered nachos, guacamole, and margaritas. After one and then two rounds of margaritas, our stories about lost relationships turned into lists of what we wanted in our next mate.

"Someone who is working on their shit," she said.

"Yup…Good in bed."

"Absolutely… Funny."

"I do like a man who makes me laugh…. Editor."

She looked at me with eyebrows raised, "That's not going to happen."

"Mario was an amazing editor – not just grammatically, but he kept me from writing shit that got me in trouble."

"I don't think you can find that."

"It's staying on my list. It may be the holy grail, but I want it." I wanted to tell her that Patrick had edited my *Elephant Journal* article. But was worried she'd think badly of me.

"If you want writing help, you should reach out to my writing coach. She's amazing."

She picked up her phone to send me the contact info. Which gave me time to look at mine. Dan had texted.

Maybe I *wouldn't* follow Mario to the grave.

\*

On Wednesday morning I walked out of the hut to see men with wheelbarrows shoveling seaweed. The piles towered over them, and the heat was so oppressive that they had to wipe their dripping foreheads with their shirts.

I saw them when I went to breakfast and again on the way

to yoga. That afternoon, one passed while I sunned on a wooden lounge chair. It felt wrong to be still while they worked so hard.

I looked down at my phone to find a text from Sienna. She was having bad stomach cramps and bleeding when she went to the bathroom. Thinking it might be food poisoning, I suggested she go to the University Health Center. She got an appointment later that afternoon.

At dinner she called to say they were taking her to the hospital. I left the restaurant and grabbed my computer from our hut. The hotel lobby had better WiFi so I went there to look for airplane tickets home. I didn't want her to go through this alone. But it was a popular vacation week and there were no direct flights. Connections would take days. I called Hope, who lived nearby, and asked her to meet Sienna at the hospital.

Later that night I spoke to Sienna's doctor. He said they could calm the bleeding, but her initial tests showed the issue wasn't food poisoning. She needed to see a specialist. I asked what it could be – my mind was already dreading the worst. *Cancer? I couldn't lose her too!*

He said it might only be an allergy, but he wasn't a specialist.

Samantha came to sit with me in the lobby. "What's going on?" she asked. I told her.

"Is there anything you can do now?"

"No. I can't get any flights there. My friend is with her at the hospital. She'll go home tonight."

"That's good."

"I feel awful. She was there for me with Mario and now I'm here when she needs me."

"I'm so sorry. It must be hard to be so far away."

"It is. I've lost so much – I don't know if I could survive losing her too." My voice broke and Samantha hugged me. We walked back to our hut. I texted Sienna and Hope into the early hours of the morning.

At some point, I fell asleep.

*

I woke to an early text from Hope saying Sienna had been discharged and was staying with her. They'd had a long night at the hospital and she was still asleep.

Later, as I watched the sunrise from the beach, I noticed pathways through the black seaweed to the ocean – and green pieces peaking out here and there.

Sienna called when she woke up around noon to say she was feeling better. She wanted to eliminate gluten from her diet because the doctor said she could be allergic to it. I mentioned that the week of largely vegetarian, gluten-free food and less wine had made a big difference for me too.

I didn't tell her about the EFT treatment with Sandra or how facing the pain and guilt head-on had lightened my suffering.

That was something I wanted to share in person.

*

By Saturday, the black seaweed was gone. Except for a few scars of black around the beach edges, it looked like it had never been there.

I packed, said goodbye to the retreaters and Samantha, and headed to the airport alone. After purchasing a few souvenirs, I wrestled my book pages from the bottom of my suitcase. I found a blue editing pen in my purse and started reading.

A few pages in, I emailed the writing coach Samantha recommended. It was time to re-tell our story.

The ending had changed.

# Chapter Thirty-One

# THE GRIEF HERD

On a chilly Saturday morning in April, I parked the Mini Cooper in front of a large banner that said YOGA. Grabbing my mat bag, meditation chair, computer, and knitting from the trunk, I headed toward the door. I noticed a few students ahead of me and turned back as if I'd forgotten something. When the coast was clear, I hurried inside to my first yoga therapy training class since Mario died.

The classroom was nearly empty as students were still in the bathroom or storing their lunches in the kitchen. I found an open space in the farthest corner from the front and dumped my stuff. Gaze down, I gathered two blankets, bolsters, and blocks from the prop area and carried them to my spot.

Settling into a comfortable seat, I looked across the room. A thin woman with long frizzy dark hair embellished with one grey streak walked toward me. She was wearing an embroidered white gauze top and tie-dye leggings. She knelt and wrapped her arms around my back. I leaned in and let my head rest on her shoulder.

When we pulled away, I could see her eyes were shiny and wet. "I'm so sorry, Donna."

I swallowed and said, "Thank you, Laura." Early in my relationship with Mario, we'd realized through Facebook that Mario and Laura had gone to the same high school. I looked around for a tissue box. Other yoga students piled into the room and some interrupted us by kneeling and hugging me. I said thank you each time, but wanted to push them away. Like a new yoga student - resisting adjustment.

Laura kept talking. "He was such a great guy. Even back in high school."

"It's so good to have you here," I said. "Because you knew him. And this really sucks." Those words reverberated into the wave of silence in the room. I looked up to see Yoga Rob sitting cross-legged with his eyes closed. Laura touched my shoulder and walked to her mat.

The room was full now – twenty-five students on yoga mats with prop piles similar to mine. Some glanced over as the lecture began. I lowered my eyes and pulled out my knitting.

*

When we broke for lunch, I grabbed my computer and went onto Facebook to host my *Elephant Journal Academy* writing group. As with yoga, the fundamentals of the writing school are Buddhist tenets like, "May it be of benefit" or "Challenges are here to teach us."

"Hello." I wrote into the Facebook group message prompt. "How is everyone today?"

"Hello, Donna. How are you?"

"Good, Francois, how was your week?"

We discussed the meditation and writing lecture *Elephant Journal* founder Waylon Lewis led that week, and Francois asked some questions. Four other students messaged hellos and there was brief chit-chat about the weather, recent travel, and the meditation class.

One student wrote, "Donna, we're so happy you decided to keep leading this group."

"Thank you. Being with you is a gift right now." And it was. The *Elephant Journal* community was there for me when Mario passed. They kept in touch frequently and encouraged me to write through my grief. I couldn't wait to thank them in person at a meet-up planned for July.

The chatter stopped. I wrote, "Now let's do five minutes of meditation. We'll start with an extended exhale practice. Breathe in and then exhale for twice as long. Keep doing that slower and slower. I'll set the timer and be back in five minutes."

Shortly, the alarm on my phone went off and I messaged, "Time's up. How does everyone feel?"

"Amazing."

"Calm."

"Tranquil."

I smiled. "Good, let's start class." We discussed the week's lecture and the assignment to post their journalism piece for feedback. Then we moved to the writing prompt.

*Write what comes to mind when you hear this Albert Camus quote, "What doesn't kill you makes you stronger..."*

One student wrote *We fail at some things, and we learn from it and overcome it the next time we face it. I love this quote!!*

Another wrote, *What doesn't kill you makes you stronger, unless it's cancer and it slowly and painfully kills you.* I made a note to follow up with her after class.

My prompt response was, *This idea keeps hitting me deeper and deeper over time. And I guess that's why it resonates. As we age, we experience more and more. And at times will be knocked over. But each time I rise I feel growth – and hopefully help others by writing about it.*

As I read through the later responses, I sent this one a smiley face with heart eyes. *Life does not get easier, but you learn how to react better to it. In time, you learn where the sugar is hidden so that you can make the best lemonade.*

My attention shifted when a yoga student came into the room. Others followed. "Time to wrap up," I messaged the writing group. "Thank you everyone. Talk to you next week unless you need me in between." I turned off my laptop and stored it away.

As always when I write, it felt like no time had passed.

*

The following day, a sympathy card from the yoga students was waiting for me in the middle of my mat. I don't remember any of the kind interior messages. Only this snarky one, "Wow, that knitting project must be so fascinating." It felt like a stab.

Maybe the person was miffed. After all I was surrounded by yogis training to assist those in pain, yet I was ignoring them as much as they'd let me. Why? Was I afraid to show weakness?

Or was I still unable to trust anyone?

*

As I drove to work the following Tuesday morning, I told Michelle about the yoga training weekend. "I just didn't want to talk about it. Especially after they kept looking at me like I had two heads when I said I was fine. I am fine. Unlike Mario's kids, my daily life hasn't been impacted by his death. I still have a job and my own kids to take care of. And since we didn't end up getting married or even living together, most of my life is the same."

"But you lost someone who loved and nurtured you."

Tears filled my eyes and my shoulders drooped. "Yeah, that happened. Maybe I'm screwing up this grief thing. I don't want to make it last longer or make myself sick from messing it up."

"I don't think you can mess it up. But maybe a grief counselor would help."

She gave me the number of one associated with the hospital where Mario was first taken after his stroke. I told her I would give them a call. Even though I doubted it would help.

*

I hate freezing rain, but on the day of the grief counselor appointment, it felt appropriate. The GPS directions took me past the hospital where Mario last talked to me. Would I ever drive by without thinking of him?

At the counselor's office, a tall middle-aged woman with red reading glasses and shoulder-length blonde hair greeted me. Her name was Lisa. She smiled and gestured toward a chair that looked like my grief chair. Her serene expression made it hard to believe she'd ever experienced grief.

Lisa let me babble for a while about yoga therapy and my *Elephant Journal* articles on grief. When I took a breath, she looked down at her yellow legal pad and asked if I read any books about grief. I mentioned the titles I could remember. I didn't mention that I'd tried to read a grief memoir by Joan Didion but found it too sad.

As we talked, I began feeling sure of myself. Like I had this grief thing under control.

And then she asked, "How did he die?" That question tore off my candy-coated surface and tears melted down my cheeks.

She passed me tissues and said I didn't have to go on, but I wanted to. I told her about the Reiki training. And the speaking in tongues at his deathbed – something I'd never told anyone else about. It had comforted me to see Mario's spirit ascending. It meant he was still with me.

She didn't seem at all surprised. "I'm a Reiki practitioner too. We find energy healing and awareness helpful for both patients and their families." Lisa looked down at her notes and asked, "How're you sleeping?"

"Okay. I have a sleeping pill prescription I can use when I can't get back to sleep."

"That's good. Sleep and regular meals are our friends when we're grieving. Are you wallowing or feeling depressed?"

"Yes. And sometimes I miss my mother. She died in November."

She looked up from her notes with wide eyes, "Oh, Donna, I didn't realize your mom died recently, too."

I started to sniffle. "Yeah. We weren't close though."

She didn't follow up on that last thread. Instead she said, "In our upcoming grief group there are several people who have had multiple deaths in a short time."

"It would be good to talk to them. Because I don't know how to do this right. And I don't have anyone in my life that has lost their husband. My sister calls a lot to check on me, but I hear the fear in her voice. In my best friend's too. Even my therapist – she's been married for decades. But my mother could have helped. She was a widow for almost thirty years." I had trouble speaking. The losses were piling up on me like cars on the turnpike.

Lisa gave me a moment to recover and didn't hug me or try to hush me with words. She just gave me space. Just like at the Kripalu sharing circle. When I breathed normally again, she asked if we could continue. I nodded.

"Are you isolating yourself?"

"In the beginning I couldn't leave the house. But eventually had to go back to work. Then I started going to restaurants – although I have yet to go to our breakfast place or the steakhouse that was our favorite dinner spot."

"Some people want to go to the places they went with their lost loved ones. Some avoid them."

Feeling a little more comfortable, I said "No one knows how to talk to me. They tell me how sorry they are, but I don't want to talk about it."

"That's why it's important to be around others experiencing similar things. I would usually suggest you wait a little longer to join a grief group. But since you are working with a therapist, you might be ready."

"Ok. Thank you for letting me try."

"You're welcome." She looked up. I turned around to see a large clock on the wall behind me. "Our time is coming to an end. If you have any questions after you leave, please email or call."

Although I've been in therapy for decades, the abrupt ending of sessions still surprises me. I put my coat on and grabbed my purse. Lisa walked with me to the exit and I carefully navigated the slippery sidewalk to my car.

Once inside, I put my head down on the wheel. I thought I was getting better, but everything was churned up again.

Eventually the tears receded, and I made my way home.

*

That night I couldn't sleep. I wrote in my journal:

His hand a gift in sleep

His kiss an exquisite alarm

I miss it all

even the snoring

\*

The following morning, I was in the bathroom getting ready for work and Michelle was on the speaker phone. "I feel so lonely. There's a big man-hole in my life where Mario was," I said, curling my eyelashes. "But the idea of dating someone else scares me. What if I break down in the middle of a date with Dan because I miss Mario? I feel like I'm cheating even thinking about someone else."

"Maybe you'll meet someone at the grief group. Then you'll have that in common."

"Maybe. But I'm scared to do that, too. I feel stuck behind a giant wall of resistance about it."

"That's normal. By going, you'll be facing the loss. I hate to mention it, but my next client is due in five minutes."

"I never seem to be able to end on time these days."

\*

On the day of the grief group, I passed the hospital again. I pushed back the image of Mario lying on a gurney, his right arm flailing.

It was 5:45 p.m. when I parked in front of the hospice center. I picked up my phone and swiped through Facebook and Instagram posts for a few minutes. Then gathered my purse and the re-purposed school composition book on which I'd written *GRIEF.*

Inside the bright and sterile classroom, I sat in an empty seat near a Kleenex box. The chair was metal, with no padding.

At precisely six o'clock, Lisa closed the door to the room.

*

She introduced herself and gave a little background about her training. Then said, "I commend you for coming today. You're taking an important step in your loss journey." I felt a sob rise in my throat. A woman a few chairs down started to weep.

Lisa pulled out a paper from her file folder and held it up like a poster. "A few rules for the group," she read. "The first few times coming here can be very hard. So, our first rule is we want you to come a couple times before deciding if this is for you."

"Second, this is a safe place. It's like Vegas. What's said here stays here. Third, we will tell our loss stories today, but after that we're going to focus on tools to recover. Four, be respectful to each other. No interrupting and no giving advice unless asked. Sound good?"

We all nodded.

"Good. So, I'm going to ask you to share your loss stories and what you're hoping to get out of this group. We aren't going to go in any order, but instead speak up like popcorn – share your story when you're ready. Or don't share at all. I've had people come to grief groups for the entire ten sessions and never share a thing. That's okay."

The room went silent. Lisa waded in, "So anyone want to go first?"

The stories spilled forth. Most of the attendees had lost their loved ones years ago. And each time they told their stories I cried a little for my own.

With minutes left in the session, I spoke. "My fiancé died earlier this year of a massive stroke. And my mother three months before that." One woman let out a small cry of surprise. Others looked at me with sympathy. I almost shared never getting over Daddy's death but didn't think I could keep going if I did. "I came here to figure out how to move on. Sometimes I wish I could follow them, but I have two kids and two dogs. They need me." I couldn't continue. Lisa looked me in the eyes to see if I had anything more to say. I shook my head no.

"Thank you, Donna." There was only one more person's story after mine. And another person didn't share at all – which I could understand. But I was glad I did. It made me feel a little lighter and less alone.

"Now that we've shared our stories, I want to take a moment to ask what you noticed."

Several people raised their hands and made comments, but they didn't seem to offer what Lisa was looking for. I raised my hand. "Yes?" she said.

"No story was the same, but we all have felt hopeless and lonely. And we want to move on."

"Yes. Exactly. Grief comes in all shapes and sizes, but the impact on the person is very similar. And because of that similarity, some tools can help. Two of which I will give you now."

Always a good student, I picked up my pen and opened my composition book.

"One of the tools to use when you're down is to change your location. Go outside or to another room. It's amazing how a new space can lighten the mood."

"Kind of what we used to do for our kids when they had the croup. We would take them outside," I said. Some nodded.

"Second, try to connect to your loved ones through happy

memories. Which is what we will focus on next meeting. Your assignment will be to bring a picture of your loved one and tell us about them. What were they like? How did they connect with you? What made you love them?" I wrote down this assignment and noted that it sounded like Sandra's advice in Tulum. Connect through happy memories.

Lisa stood up and said, "Our time is up. If you need to reach me, please email or call. See you next week."

We burst from the room and those that could sprinted to their cars. It was like being released from a class we hated but needed to graduate.

I wondered if I could.

*

Two weeks later, I was in the Wawa getting a sixteen-ounce hazelnut coffee with French vanilla cream when my phone rang. Looking down, I saw Michelle calling. I was late – again. I swiped to answer.

"Hey, sorry I'm late. I'm at Wawa getting coffee."

"That's okay. You do like your Wawa."

"Yes. Routine is everything for me these days."

"I get that. How're things?"

"Not great. I keep having crying and raging fits. Yesterday I got an offer in the mail asking if I wanted to trade in the seven-passenger SUV I bought to fit our kids. I got so angry. Here I am with this huge vehicle for a family life that died with Mario."

"You should have reached out to me."

"I know. I did call Sienna. She's a great listener.

"You worked hard on that relationship."

"I have. I should probably trade it in but can't. I'm having trouble letting go of his things – like the clothes that still smell of him or the sushi pillow he gave me to celebrate his win at getting me to like sushi. I hate that pillow. It's hideous. But it's not going anywhere."

"Donna, *of course* you're angry. Look at what you've been through."

I took a deep breath and felt the exhale soften everything. "Thank you. Those two words made me feel so much better."

"You are always trying so hard. Sometimes you need to give yourself a break."

"It's tough to do that. Or to be vulnerable. Hearing you say *of course* about the anger I was kicking myself for is such a gift."

"Yeah – they call that New Age Guilt." She explained that time spent in therapy and self-discovery can lead us to believe we are beyond basic emotions. But everyone gets triggered. It's part of being human.

"New Age Guilt. I'll have to remember that."

"What did you do this week?"

"Some old friends came to visit."

"That sounds nice."

"It should've been. But I feel like I'm on some funeral tour. Where everyone comes to check on me. They mean well, but they keep telling me it's for the best, or asking me to tell the story of what happened. It doesn't feel like the best right now and I don't want to relive things anymore."

"That must be hard."

"It is. So last week I asked Patrick to come along as a friend buffer. To prevent the discussion from sliding into all things death."

"How did it feel to be out with him?"

"Good. Natural. He's so calm and kind. And he never embarrasses me. I feel like I can take him anywhere."

"You haven't always had that. Must have felt good."

"It did." I pulled into the garage at work and parked.

"How was the grief group?"

I told her that after a couple of meetings I wasn't finding it helpful. We were doing the same work in our sessions. And sometimes it felt worse to listen to others in pain.

Besides, Sienna was coming home for a few weeks to complete some medical tests for her stomach issues. And I wanted to spend as much time with her as possible before she left for her summer internship.

*

The Saturday after Sienna got home from school, I picked up Mario's kids and we all went to lunch. We had kept in touch through Diana - but had yet to get together in person. It had been too hard for them till now. I understood.

We chose the restaurant where everyone met for the first time, the one where kids eat free. I could almost hear Mario saying that.

When the waitress asked how many, I paused and said, "Six." She grabbed menus and walked us to a table by the bathroom.

After the initial awkwardness of being together without him, we got on like nothing terrible had happened. His daughter played tic-tac-toe with Sienna and the boys showed Sylvie YouTube videos. There was an ease in their interaction - maybe because we were the only ones who knew how each other felt. And no one mentioned *who* was missing.

At one point as the kids ate, talked, and teased, I fell silent. We would have been an amazing family. Now we were just the people who loved and missed him the most.

*

After we dropped off Mario's kids, Sienna said, "We still need this SUV after all – to drive everyone."

My eyes filled. "Yup. You're so smart."

"Of course. I'm your daughter." She shrugged her shoulders and moved her hands into the "whatever" emoji sign and smiled.

At that moment, the song "I Like Me Better When I'm With You" came on the radio. I had taken it out of my yoga playlists because it reminded me of Mario – how he made me a better person. But hearing it today felt like he was with me. I tapped my fingers on the steering wheel and swayed my head to the music. My daughters joined in.

When we got home, I went upstairs to the bedroom and pulled out the jewelry box with the engagement ring Mario had given me. The mother's ring with a stone for each of our five children.

We were still bound together – as his grief herd.

*Chapter Thirty-Two*

# THIS YOGA SHIT REALLY WORKS

I squinted at the digital clock on the nightstand. 12:15 a.m. Sunday. Why was my stomach aching, my head a concrete block? Then the replay from the night before rolled. Me sitting in front of a *Shahs of Sunset* marathon drinking more than my daily quota of wine and eating whatever sweet or crunchy food I could find. No one was around to see me. Sylvie was at her dad's and Mario was dead.

Walking to the bathroom, I opened the cabinet door where his medications still were. I pulled out a medicated headache strip and put it on my forehead. My bangs got caught in it, so I reapplied. Blessed coolness numbed everything.

I snuggled back under the covers and closed my eyes. A few moments later I picked up my always ready journal, and wrote:

*Why am I doing this? I don't want to go on this date with Dan today. But I've put him off as long as I can. And I can't go through another Sunday alone!*

My chest tightened and there was tingling on the back of my head. Yogi walked from the foot of the bed to my face and curled up.

244

Jake launched from the blue grief chair onto the bed and snuggled behind me.

I looked at the three books by my bedside. All too sad or frivolous.

Switching on the TV to Bravo, I saw Bethenny Frankel crying over her divorce. My eyes closed. I used to think that was the worst that could happen too.

\*

When I parked in the underground parking garage ten hours later, the clock showed I was fifteen minutes early.

I started swiping through Facebook posts when a text came through. "I'm here. Black Toyota Camry." It was Dan.

Mario had a Camry too. Tan. A swish of sadness burned through my chest. "Be right there," I texted. I looked at my face in the rearview mirror, pulled out a neutral lipstick, applied it, and got out. Closing the door, I noticed the sound echoing across the garage.

I could see Dan standing next to his car. How tall he was. Six-foot-two and all legs. He was wearing a pair of black jeans and a dark purple long-sleeved shirt with a print on the inside collar. I'd bought similar shirts for Jim from an expensive big and tall shop.

Even though there were no cars on the street this early, I looked left and right before crossing. Dan was smiling. I forced a grin.

After we got in his car, he locked the doors. I quickly examined the latch. Dan kept smiling. Sweat dripped down my arm.

He placed his hands on the steering wheel and said, "I'm taking us to The Whip for brunch. It's your favorite restaurant, right?"

"It is. You remembered." Which would have been great, but the last time I was there was with Mario and our kids. My left knee started to tremble. I put my hand on it. It stopped.

"I also made a playlist for the drive. Some songs I like and songs from bands you said you liked."

"Wow. What bands did you pick?" What should have been a charming gesture made me feel guilty. Hopefully, he hadn't gone to too much trouble.

"It'll be a surprise." He started off with a song from Kansas - one of Mario's oldest son's favorite bands. And then moved on to Pink Floyd's "The Wall." I told him I liked them. Although the band's heavy drug and anti-school themes have always been a little disturbing.

"The next one's for you," he said. Coldplay's "Viva La Vida" came on. "Do you like it?"

"I do. I remember listening to it as I traveled, explaining awful investment returns to clients during the Great Recession."

"Sounds fun," he said. "I thought you were a project manager?"

"I am now. Then I was working in sales for an investment manager. But project management let me be home more after the divorce."

"I get that."

"Yeah, and the money wasn't worth the stress and time away."

"Project management is what I do too. I like it, but it can be stressful at times."

I agreed, even though I found it a little dull.

*

My favorite thing about The Whip is its location. It's snuggled within Chester County's horse country, about thirty minutes from where I grew up. To get there you must navigate windy roads, one-car covered bridges, and the occasional wayward cow or horse-drawn buggy.

When we got close, I looked for my tree – a lone grand maple on a hill. I'd long wondered why someone planted it in the middle of a field, all alone. And how it managed to grow so tall with no others to shelter it from storms. I showed it to Jim and the kids, then Mario. We always looked for it when we were together.

As we rounded a turn, it appeared. Stately, tall, and full of light green leaves.

I smiled but said nothing.

*

When we arrived at the restaurant there was a line, so we gave the hostess our name and turned to the seating area near the bar. Long built-in benches and low coffee tables were adorned with checkers and other games. Some elementary school-age kids were playing with them. Dan asked if I wanted something to drink. I asked for a Corona and sat in an open space by the window.

He got an IPA and sat next to me. The area was crowded with multi-generational families. Daughters, mothers, and grandparents. I noticed their wedding and engagement bands. And my empty fingers.

Flat screens over the bar were showing soccer games. Dan commiserated with some of the men about the scores while I watched the kids play checkers. We could have been like everyone else. If only my knee would stop shaking.

Eventually they called Dan's name and we were shown to a four-seater table by the wall. The same booth I'd been in with Mario a year or so before. I wiped my eyes with a napkin, put it on my lap, and took a sip from the Corona.

Did Uber pick up from here? Then I remembered Sylvie's first question to any Whip waitress was, "What's the WiFi code?" because there's no cell service.

The place is known for its English fare, so when the server came I asked for fish and chips with coleslaw and Dan ordered something similarly English and unhealthy. After she left, we talked about our Mexico and hiking vacations. I don't remember much after that or returning to the car. I do remember his hand finding my left knee on the drive home. Maybe he noticed it shaking. It didn't feel overly sexual, but I jumped so high my stomach dug into the seatbelt. He pulled back to put both hands on the wheel for a turn. Pink Floyd's "Wish You Were Here" came on.

I imagined Mario was driving.

We listened without speaking until we arrived at the garage. I jumped out of the car before he could open his door, then reached my arms high to hug him.

"Can we get together again?" he asked as we pulled apart.

I was surprised. Had I gotten so good at pretending to be okay that he didn't notice the sadness? That I shouldn't be dating at all? That I was still in love with another man?

Who was no longer available.

I said, "Sure" even though I knew continuing this was foolish.

He offered to walk me to my car, but I said, "That's okay," and turned away, ensuring no end-of-date kiss. I felt terrible and spun back to say, "Thanks for today."

He smiled and got into his car.

When I drove out of the garage a few minutes later, the black Camry was gone.

\*

On an overcast day in late April, Sienna and I parked in front of the local outpatient hospital. As we entered I was immediately overwhelmed by the smell of antiseptic.

"The smell reminds me of Mario," Sienna said. It's freaky how she reads my mind.

The registration attendant gave us forms to fill out. I put on my reading glasses. My hand was shaking so I used capital letters. Daddy always used capital letters.

They called her name and we both went back. While Sienna went to the bathroom to change into her gown, I talked with the nurse. I told her how we were a bit skittish because my fiancé had died from a stroke in February. That we were in the hospital with him when it happened. She said how sorry she was and reassured me that the colonoscopy would be easy. That the worst part was the preparation. I wanted to believe her.

Through the curtains around the bed, I could see other patients. They all had grey hair and a few had canes. Sienna was the youngest by far. I was a close second.

When she returned, they told us what would happen during the colonoscopy and even though we'd read everything about it online, we listened as if there was going to be a test. The anesthesiologist came to put an IV in her left hand. I held her right hand and closed my eyes, then put my head down so I wouldn't faint.

Within minutes, Sienna was drowsy. I kissed her on the forehead and watched as her eyes flickered and closed. A doctor talked to me while the nurses unlocked the brakes on Sienna's bed. I don't remember what he said. I was too busy watching them roll my life away.

*

As I waited in the operating room lobby, *Flea Market Flip* came on HGTV. Even though it seemed like the decorating channel was always on in hospitals, the show comforted me because Mario and I used to watch it together. Within two episodes the nurse came to take me back. The procedure was over.

When I first saw Sienna, her skin was pale and her eyes were closed. When they opened, she smiled. "Mama, I talked to Mario while I was asleep." I kissed the top of her head.

"You did? What did he say?"

"I don't remember. But it was good to see him." I hugged her and asked the nurse for crackers and ginger ale.

As she ate the snack, I told her the story about Mario insisting we get married after his back surgery.

*

A few days later, we got Sienna's results. One of the blood tests indicated a gluten allergy. All the late-night pizza and wine during and after Mario's illness had taken a toll on us both. We decided to listen to our bodies and eliminate what wasn't working. To face our grief without the usual numbing mechanisms.

There were lots of stops and starts. But eventually we began to heal.

*

On a Sunday in June, I parked under a blooming cherry blossom tree and loaded up my yoga bag, meditation chair, and knitting. I opened the door and let a woman wearing neon leggings and a shirt that said "Namaste Right Here" go in ahead of me. We were late.

"Aren't you excited? This is your last day of yoga therapy training, right?" she asked as we hurried through the lobby.

"Yes. I'm a little sad, but mostly happy."

"I bet. Wish I was finishing this year, but I have a whole 'nother to go."

We rushed up the stairs and kicked off our shoes in the cubby area. She split for the front of the studio, and as usual I aimed for the back. Pushing the door open made a plucking sound that resonated across the container of silence. The same redheaded leader from the trauma-aware workshop put a finger to her mouth as I walked in.

Every space across the floor and along the walls was full. Nearly everyone was meditating. A woman gestured "I'll make a space." I set my meditation chair near her. Within minutes a bell chimed three times to signal the end of meditation practice. The leader barely let the sound fade before quarreling with the computer and video projector. Finally, she displayed a slide on the wall.

She took a deep breath and said, "Today we're going to discuss karma. What do you think when you hear the word karma?" Hands raised. "Yes, Chelsea?"

"What goes around comes around."

"Yes, that's what most people think. But it's a lot more than that. Anyone else? Over in the corner – Lydia?"

"The energy that we put out in the universe comes back to us."

"Yes, that's part of it too. But there's more. Anyone else?"

I raised my hand. "Isn't karma just the sum of our decisions? A therapist once said to me, you marry your most neurotic parent. In this case my mother. But as I started healing from childhood, I realized my marriage didn't work anymore. So, we got divorced. Of course, he cheated on me which made that easier." There were some laughs and comments.

"That description misses the energetic and historic part of karma," the teacher said. "Karma is the sum of a person's actions in this and previous states of existence, which then decides their fate in future existences. It can be karma you create, or it can be karma you carry from your parents' and other predecessors' actions."

"So, it's not only what I've done, but what I carry with me from my parents or others?" I asked.

"Yes. And since you brought it up, your husband probably married you because he was looking to work out karma from childhood or a past life."

I slowly smiled, "You mean I was a bad choice for him?"

She nodded. "Possibly, yes."

"He would agree with you." I laughed and listened as others in the class started asking questions.

I wrote the definition of karma and her comments in my multi-colored patchwork notebook. Other students' hands popped up and more karma stories were told. I swiped my phone open at a text from Patrick asking me to dinner the following week. But before responding I heard the teacher say, "And before we can burn the karma of past experiences away, there is usually a period of stress where everything in our lives comes apart. To shake us aware."

I wrote that down and underlined it and added, *I wonder if the divorce and Mother's and Mario's deaths were not just bad luck but burning karma. A chance to practice what I've learned.*

*If so, I'm not going to waste it.*

*

Later, as the afternoon sun streamed into the studio, Yoga Rob asked us to gather in a circle. Those graduating were to give a brief speech. As everyone shared, we laughed, cried, and observed moments of silence.

When they got to me, I said, "People come up to me all the time and ask how I am doing so well after all I've been through. I tell them I leaned heavily on what I learned here."

Yoga was like a "gateway practice" for me. It helped me release childhood trauma and led me to Sandra's EFT treatment, which freed both the guilt and grief after Mario died. Without yoga, I would never have found *Elephant Journal* or encountered Reiki, which let me see Mario's ongoing presence in our lives. And practicing yoga and meditation helped me face my feelings instead of numbing them, which led to a healthier relationship with food and alcohol.

I smiled and wrapped up with, "This yoga shit really works."

*

On a warm summer evening, I parked my car at the garage in town and walked up the stairs toward Limoncello Restaurant. For this non-date, I'd picked a high-cut blue-and-white-striped cotton maxi dress with low slits that showed my legs. I smiled as my gold flip-flops clipped along the brick sidewalk. I felt more like myself than I had in months.

I walked down the row of wicker umbrella tables outside the restaurant, and was about to turn around when I heard, "Donna, are you meeting someone else?"

Laughing out loud, I turned to see Patrick seated with a ginger ale in front of him. He looked so handsome in a blue striped button-down shirt and jeans, and his hair and beard looked recently trimmed. He stood and pulled my chair out.

After the waiter took our drink orders, we caught up on how our day had gone. I complimented him on the restaurant choice. He said he'd picked it because it had a salmon dish – my favorite. I thanked him for remembering.

When the food came, we ate and talked for over an hour. No memories of Mario visited. And my knee remained still.

After dinner we walked to my car. I offered to drive him to his house. He accepted. It was a quiet drive, but I wasn't concerned. He'd told me when we'd dated before that sometimes he tries to out-silence people. It comes naturally because he's shy. Determined not to be outdone, I stayed quiet too. I could do that now.

I parked the car outside his house, but he didn't make a move to get out. We sat for a moment. I was about to give in and break the silence when he said, "Can I tell you something?"

I hesitated. We were just friends. What could it hurt? "Sure."

"Remember our first date at the gelato place when you asked me, 'What's next?'"

"I think so."

"I've been thinking about this for a long time, and I wish I'd said, 'We live happily ever after.'"

I was speechless. My eyes narrowed. "What do you mean?" It had been so long ago for me, and so much had happened in between. I couldn't believe he was bringing this up now.

"I know you're still grieving. And I don't want to push you. But I made a mistake letting you go before. And I don't want to do that again."

"But you dumped me because I was getting out of a twenty-year marriage. You said it was too soon. That I wasn't ready, because I was going through too many transitions."

"I know. I was wrong. I've regretted it since. And worried you might get away again."

I turned to face him, pushing my back into the driver's side door. Maybe he did know I was on *Our Time*. "But this is worse. I didn't love my husband then, so the divorce was easy compared to this. I'm devastated."

"I know."

"I'm afraid you'll just leave me again because I'm not ready." My eyes blurred. "And I don't know if I can stand to lose another man in my life."

"I'm not going anywhere."

"How can I believe that after last time?"

"I'll just have to prove it to you."

I didn't know what to say. But my body was telling me to flee. "I need to get home to let the dogs out."

He was silent for a moment. Then said, "I understand."

I gave him a quick hug and he got out of the car. As I drove away, I looked back to see him. Waving from the sidewalk.

*Chapter Thirty-Three*

# SLOUGHING OFF THE GUNK

Soon after the dinner with Patrick I broke things off with Dan and removed my profile from *Our Time*. I told him I was seeing someone I'd dated a few years ago. That we were giving it another chance. Though that wasn't the whole truth.

I did want to try again with Patrick, eventually. But I wasn't ready. Not because it was wrong or somehow disrespectful. But because I needed to sit with the pain of losing Mario – and all my other "stuff."

I had run out of runway. Escape was no longer an option. I had to feel it all.

It wasn't easy. But like in yoga, practice makes it possible.

\*

As for Patrick, when we'd first met I still wanted drama, and his quiet contemplation was unfamiliar and uncomfortable. Now I felt at ease in silence, even craved it. And experience and time had softened him too.

At first, our outings were walks in his neighborhood or trips to the movies. He respected my desire for companionship and didn't press for more.

Our early time together gave me a glimpse of what it could be like if I weren't grieving. If I were happier. It let me imagine another life. One where I hadn't lost so much and everyone didn't feel sorry for me (including me).

Even though it might have been too soon (again), losing Mario made me realize life was too precious, too short to wait for the day I was perfectly over his loss. I worried what people would think, but did what I wanted. Needed.

After several months, our relationship deepened and, although it took a while, I forgave him for letting me go the first time. Partly because that pause in our relationship gave me Mario – and I would never have wanted to miss out on that. But also I realized he gave me up because I wasn't good for him then. And that kind of self-love is something I admire and want in my life.

We spent most days and nights apart because our dogs weren't compatible. Or at least that's what we told each other. Either way, the solitude gave me time to heal and get used to being alone. And enjoy it.

Slowly the weight of grief lessened. It didn't fill every day, just some days. When the waves hit, I would put on Mario's clothes, take hot baths, and stay in bed reading, writing, and watching HGTV or the Steelers until the storm passed.

\*

On a gloomy morning in late September, I parked my car in front of the now permanently closed minimart. The Wawa next door had finally put it out of business.

I texted Patrick to let him know I was going to be in Reiki class until noon. He texted back telling me to have fun. And that he loved me. I smiled and replied the same.

Walking up the worn wooden stairs to the wellness studio, I

retrieved a tissue from my pocket and wiped my nose, then entered.

The teacher, Maria, was sitting at the small desk by the door talking to a student. The room's moss green walls, foggy fountain, and hardwood floors felt like a hug. I noticed metal chairs in a half-circle toward the back of the room. A couple of women were already there. One reminded me of Lily Tomlin's hippie character on *Grace and Frankie*, the Netflix show. The other wore brown leggings with a long tie-dyed shirt that said "Breathe." Her blonde highlighted hair was in a ponytail. They looked up and smiled. I smiled back.

When Maria was free, I stepped in front of the desk and greeted her in a raspy voice. She asked if I had a cold, and I mentioned I hadn't been sick like this since the Reiki I training in January.

"That's part of the preparation process," she said. "Your body is sloughing off emotional and spiritual gunk so you can do the training."

"That makes perfect sense." And it did. I wanted to ask her about scheduling a psychic reading but was self-conscious in front of everyone, so decided to ask later.

After paying for the class, I sat in the metal chair closest to the door. Maria asked everyone to introduce themselves. The student in the "Breathe" shirt said she was a medium.

When it was my turn I said, "My name is Donna and I'm a yoga teacher by night and a corporate project manager by day. I took Reiki I training to enhance my yoga classes, and it's taken me this long to take Reiki II training because a couple weeks after taking the first training my fiancé had a massive stroke. He eventually died."

One woman brought her hands up to her face in shock. The medium said, "He's behind you. His hand is on your shoulder."

"Today is the anniversary of our first date." My eyes filled. "Which shoulder?"

"The left one." I put my right hand there. It felt warm.

"Thank you," I said. She nodded.

Once everyone had spoken, the teacher began the training with meditation. She followed with a lecture on how applying crystals to different chakra areas could strengthen the energy release. We tried various crystals and one – apophyllite – made all the tightness in my body relax. The rock was white with sparkles and a lead-grey bottom. At lunch, I drove to a nearby crystal shop and bought one. Today it's part of my daily energy cleansing routine.

That afternoon when the students were doing a Reiki share on the medium, she asked, "Who's at my head?"

I said it was me.

"Did your mother die recently?" she asked.

I felt pressure under my eyes. Why was Mother bothering me now? "Yes. She died almost a year ago."

"She's here."

Ugh, how annoying. If I wanted to connect with anyone it was Mario, not Mother. I ignored what was happening by focusing on the work, the Reiki. My fingers gently cradled the base of her skull.

But she kept talking, "Did your mother like to cook, wait, no, she liked to bake. Right?"

"Yes." Just like Sienna. How did she know that? To change the subject, I asked one of the students about a crystal they were holding.

But my hands grew warm. They became so hot I had to shake them to cool down. No one seemed to notice and the group conversation moved on.

Yet, I couldn't stop thinking about Mother.

What did *she* want?

*Chapter Thirty-Four*

# HE'S GOT YOUR BACK

It was abnormally warm for the Friday after Thanksgiving. Too balmy for a Christmas craft fair, but I promised a friend we'd go.

I'd just finished putting hot rollers in my hair when a ding signaled a new text. Patrick. Sending me the song of the day. But this time it was a YouTube video – "The Season's Upon Us" by the Dropkick Murphys. I texted back an enthusiastic thank you. I was feeling a little uncomfortable because I'd scheduled a psychic session with Maria. To talk about him – and Mario.

I walked to Sienna's room and woke her to ensure she'd be ready for her psychic session, scheduled right after mine. She turned over and promised to get up. Yogi licked her hand. She was taking him back to college with her. They'd both been there for me during the challenging times – and now deserved to be together.

She mentioned she was up late talking to a boy she was dating. I felt relieved. She'd been a bit of a commitment-phobe since the divorce.

I heard my cell phone ringing and ran down the hall to answer it – Maria. "Hi, Donna. Is now still a good time?"

"Yes. Sorry I was such a spaz at Master Reiki training." I'd almost fainted during the final attunement.

"Oh, it's fine. I could feel you weren't confident. But the guides wouldn't have let it happen if it wasn't meant to be."

"I guess." It was strange how scared I'd been. When I entered yoga teacher training, I was so confident. But now I knew how much there was to learn.

"When is your birthday?"

I told her, then asked impatiently, "Is Mario okay?"

"Yes. Yes. He's fine." She paused for a moment, then said, "He wants you to know he's always with you. He keeps trying to let you know he's there. He uses songs and moves objects. And birds."

I leaned back on one of the large white square pillows on my bed. "Yes. I keep seeing cardinals. He said cardinals were a way for his parents to contact him." I crisscrossed my hands palms down on my heart. "What else does he say?"

"He's sorry. Very sorry he left you so early."

My voice caught and I couldn't respond. I grabbed a tissue from the bedside table. "I really miss him."

"I know, I know. But he is with an important female person in his life."

"Maybe his mother."

"Yes. It might be his mother."

I took a drink of water. "What else is happening?"

"You have other guides that are talking. Wait a moment." She paused and then said, "They are all talking at once so I can't hear them."

The corners of my mouth lifted, "Sounds like Mario and his family."

She laughed. "Maybe. They are saying you are going through a major shift in life."

"That makes sense. Sylvie is graduating high school soon and I'm trying to figure out next steps. My new boyfriend Patrick wants me to move in with him. Should I?"

"I think you will fit together perfectly. You are both non-invasive in your lives. You don't tell each other what to do."

I wrote that down. "That's true. When we're together it's easy."

"You get respect from him and reciprocation. You haven't had this."

"I *haven't* had that. Not even with Mario because he always put his kids first. Because they were so young."

She kept going like she didn't hear me, "I don't see you staying where you are though. You want to get out of your house – you lived in it with your ex, then Mario. Too much energy."

"Okay."

"Mmmm. Then Patrick will move in with you at first, and then you will sell your place and move in together somewhere else."

Although that was not what we planned, I believed her. "So, it's going to work out?"

"Yeah. I like this guy. What's his birthday?"

I told her.

"In numerology, you both have a 2 – partnerships. Both of you are looking for partners. Don't feel right until you have someone."

"That explains a lot." And maybe why I wanted to get back out there so soon after my separation and Mario's passing.

She kept going, "You also both have 3's. So, you are both communicators. And you like to be a part of something bigger than yourselves. To help others."

"He does have an 8 – so he tends to worry about how things will go. Thoughts are intention. Teach him that. You are in his life to teach him what you know. Show him that what you put out there is what you get back."

I felt a little impatient. "Okay. But what will he teach *me*?" I poised the pen to take down her words.

"He is meant to teach you that someone actually has your back."

I wrote that down. Then put three stars next to it. I looked at the clock. Time was almost up. "Any last stuff I should ask about?"

"Do you have an older female that crossed over?"

"My mother did. She died over a year ago." Why was Mother bothering me again?

"I'm sorry."

"It was a difficult relationship."

"She loves you, but it was hard to show you. She's sorry about that. She's talking…" Maria paused for a moment, then said, "She wants to tell you how strong you've become and how proud she is of you. She's saying, 'I'm so sorry I wasn't able to give you what you needed.'"

My fingers gripped the pen. "She abused me."

"She wanted control."

"She was damaged."

"She's remorseful now. Trying to make amends."

I put the journal and pen down. "It's nice she's reaching toward me *now*, I guess." Mother had been the villain so long it was hard to see her any other way.

"It's a shame she has to do it from the other side."

I lay down on the bed. Time to change the subject. "Do you see my father at all?"

"He seems laid back and going with the flow. Was she the boss?"

"I guess – and he's been gone a long time. He died thirty years ago."

"Did he have heart issues?"

"Yes. He died of a heart attack, they think. He had a quadruple bypass when I was in college."

"He says you can do whatever you want. Dream big."

"He always believed in me." I rolled over into the fetal position.

Maria went on, "He had a tumultuous relationship with your mom. Deeply loved her. They had been together in a past life. But it was damned. He had a heart condition because he couldn't leave her."

"I wish he had saved me from her abuse."

"That's why it's so important that you have someone who has your back. Like Patrick. You crave that."

I sat up. I felt just like an HGTV reveal. Everything hidden under years of grime was tossed, transformed. Rejuvenated.

Maria asked if I was ready to turn the call over to Sienna. I hurried down the hall to hand over the phone.

Back in my bedroom I grabbed Mario's anniversary pillow and put it on my lap. Jake scootched over so he was right next to me. I hit the video link Patrick texted. In Irish brogue the song and video hilariously detailed holiday family dysfunction.

Within minutes I was laughing out loud and Jake was jumping around the room. I walked to the closet and put Mario's pillow on an upper shelf, then went downstairs to face the foyer. It was filled with unopened bins of Christmas decorations.

I opened a red plastic bin. Inside was the pink and white shoebox that held Mother's nativity set. Maybe she did love me. Not in a healthy or nurturing way, but the best way she could.

After pulling out the small wooden barn, I laid the white snow blanket of cotton batting on the dining room sideboard and placed the building on top. I pulled the rubber band off the shoebox and carefully unwrapped the nativity figures. First the camels, lambs, and sheep, then the wise men and shepherds. Finally, the baby, Mary, and Joseph. Joseph's head was still broken. I gently laid him down and walked to the kitchen to add Gorilla Glue to the grocery list.

*

It was still dark outside when I climbed into Patrick's car. Without asking, he pulled up to the nearest Wawa so I could get coffee. I hoped they still had the Christmas blend even though it was already New Year's Eve.

Patrick had already gotten his Dunkin Donuts coffee fix, but he walked inside with me anyway and held the passenger side door open when we returned.

As we drove across the Commodore Barry Bridge to New Jersey, he pointed out the sunrise so I could take a picture for my daily meme. After posting it, I looked over at his bearded and bespectacled face and noticed how safe and calm I felt. I couldn't remember feeling like this with anyone else.

As we finished the coffees, our conversation gradually gained momentum. We talked about moving in together and the trips we wanted to take.

As we talked, I sat there, still knitting the mess of a scarf that had accompanied me in Mario's hospital room, hospice room, and later kept me from making eye contact during yoga training. I had knitted the scarf on multiple drives with Patrick to meet his kids and his sister and on our trips visiting poets' graves. I was a terrible knitter, and the scarf was full of mistakes. Sometimes I wanted to burn it.

I broke a short silence by suggesting we get our kids together.

He said, "Let's keep it just us for now. Only *we* matter."

My face broke into a wide smile. "No one has ever put me first before."

He smiled back and tickled my knee with his fingers.

The weather was warm for a New Year's Eve – fifty degrees and sunny. We took Exit 0 and within ten minutes were driving beside Cape May beach. People were riding bikes and walking toward Uncle Bill's Pancake House, one of the few restaurants open year-round.

"I've come down here a lot this time of year and this is the busiest I've seen it," Patrick said.

"I've been doing this for years too."

He parked the car at the farthest end of the beach. I could see the lighthouse clearly from my window. We got out and headed toward the wooden boardwalk that led to the sand. The sun was streaming down like the touch of the divine. We took pictures and when I wasn't looking, he took one of me gazing at the sky.

We talked and waved at the other couples walking on the beach. I said how nice it was to be one of them. "You make me happy."

"I don't make you happy – you make you happy," he said. I stopped and looked at him questioningly. "But I'm glad you feel happy when you're with me."

I hugged him. How had I managed to find someone who thought like that? He was almost perfect – but how could anyone root for the New England Patriots? We separated and kept walking.

Finally, we reached the lighthouse. He pulled me close and wrapped his arms around my back as my hands found his hips. We kissed for a few moments next to the concrete army bunkers and a sign that said, "Do not climb."

I looked forward to doing *it* again.

*Chapter Thirty-Five*

# BELIEVING IN WINDMILLS

Around 10 a.m. on the Friday before the Super Bowl, I dropped Jake at the dog sitters and turned the car toward the turnpike and Kripalu. The last times I'd gone, someone else drove. This time I was going alone. Without the benefit of a friend or a bottle of wine.

The lack of wine was due to Sienna. She'd talked me into a new thirty-day health regimen that required abstaining from alcohol. She felt so great after doing it that I'd agreed to try it too.

If you are really, really, really lucky, your children become your best example.

*

Entering the turnpike, I had nowhere to be and no one to please and couldn't remember ever feeling so free. I loaded up an audiobook Sienna suggested and sipped my Wawa French vanilla coffee.

Five hours later, I passed the musty bed and breakfast where Mario and I stayed on our last visit. My eyes welled as I made the right into the Kripalu compound. I wound up the curvy path to the registration area. This place felt like a sacred and mystical home.

Even the snow embankments were white, not the mushy grey color found in West Chester.

I secured my stay with the registration clerk but was too early to check into my room. Back to the SUV. Stockbridge was calling.

As I drove through the town, I remembered Mario telling me how Norman Rockwell used Stockbridge as his inspiration. The Red Lion Inn on the right was where we'd had dinner the weekend we got engaged. I drove past the liquor store where we bought wine and cheese. Then parked in front of the Catholic church that Mario wandered into the last time we were here – the August after his mother died – the August before he died. I remember being confused by his interest in the church because, until then, we'd never entered one together.

Since his passing, I've visited many churches. Mostly with Patrick. We've attended services together and visited sanctuaries on our day trips. Inside we sit and sometimes kneel. We stare at the beautiful stained glass and absorb the spiritual energy.

You may wonder if I'm a believer. I am. A believer in love. And where love connects with religion of any kind - I'm a believer in that too.

Eventually I noticed the time and turned the SUV toward Kripalu. The registration clerk released the room key and I entered a small room with two single cots. One was so close to the door that I had to shove it aside to bring in my suitcase. I walked to the window and took a picture of the trees in the distance. I sent it to the kids. Then to Patrick.

I poked my head in the bathroom. My body cheered at the sight of a bathtub.

*

After a routine exploration of the Kripalu shop, I headed back to the room. As I entered the hallway from the fourth-floor stairwell, I saw Stephen Cope – leader of the last retreat I attended - getting off the elevator with his bags. Feeling shy, I hurried toward my room.

I could hear his footfalls behind me and felt an urge to turn around. It was like someone was pushing me. "Stephen Cope?"

He smiled and said, "Yes. You look familiar…"

"Oh sorry. My name's Donna. I took your 'The Great Work of Your Life' workshop last year."

"Yes. Yes. So good to see you. What're you here for this time?"

My shoulders drooped. "I'm here for a grief workshop."

He stopped and put down his bags. He said nothing, but his eyes asked me to continue.

"It will be a year on Sunday since my fiancé had the stroke that killed him. He was with me the last time I was here. For your retreat." My face scrunched. I was ugly crying in front of my yoga idol. I felt like a complete idiot.

He opened his arms. I stumbled into them, the straps of his backpack a barrier between us. When we pulled away, he said, "So, you're going through an anniversary."

"Oh yes," I said perking up. "I just read your *Soul Friends* book. I hope you are going to do a retreat for that book. I would definitely come."

"I'm going to," he paused and picked up his bags. "So very sorry for your loss."

"Thank you. And thank you for this – it feels right to see you as I arrive." I started walking toward my room, wanting to be cool and not take too much of an expert's time. He started walking too.

"I'm sure we'll see each other again," he said.

"I hope so." I decided right then to attend his summer retreat titled "The Practice of Loving-Kindness." He was leading it with another well-known teacher - Sharon Salzberg.

I entered my room and sat down. Then texted Patrick, "Just ran into one of my favorite authors, Stephen Cope. He's staying on my floor."

"Separate rooms, I hope. No chakra mingling."

"Aw, you used 'chakra' in a sentence."

"Don't change the subject."

"Don't worry, my love, I only mingle my chakras with you."

*

That evening I descended five flights of stairs to the workshop classroom. It was in the Annex building where Mario and I stayed when we got engaged. I swallowed hard upon entering and hid in a chair in the back row. As far from the teacher as possible.

The class started with a breathing meditation. The teacher, Maria Sirois, encouraged us to observe the breath as it came in and out of our noses. "Noticing when our thoughts wander allows us to build awareness," she said. "And that awareness can give us time to pause and reflect rather than react and be triggered. It allows us to be our best person, even in difficult situations."

Afterward, she told us stories about her "crazy" reactions to her brother's death. He died young from a rare cancer. Some of her bad habits were my own. Like drinking or overeating. She said that with meditation and awareness we could decide to stop these habitual behaviors. I hoped I could.

When we were separated into group "pods," I heard others express guilt about their lost loved ones. One was sad because she hadn't cherished them while they were alive. I told them I felt the same way.

At the end of the night, Maria said, "Instead of post-traumatic stress, some people can experience post-traumatic growth. They suffer loss and become better people as a result. New paths and relationships open for them. They thrive instead of survive. And for the next two days, we're going to learn how."

*

Two days later, I woke early on Super Bowl Sunday to a dark room. I turned on the light and pulled the *Wild Uncharted Tarot Deck* from the side table. After shuffling a few minutes, I separated the cards into three piles and re-stacked them. I selected the top card. It showed a beautiful blue-green butterfly hovering high above a tangled dusty pile of black sticks. I read the six of wands card description:

"From the dark and tangled branches emerges a butterfly... The obstacles have been relentless, but now is not the time to look back upon them. The more pressing question is: where will you go with your new set of wings?"

Where indeed? It had been a year since Mario died, fifteen months since Mother died, and almost three years since the divorce. I'd spent the weekend learning grief recovery tools – many already used. Mindfulness practices, journaling, meditation, and of course, yoga.

I could win a prize for most well-adjusted griever – if there were one. It's like I'd developed a superpower. With these tools I might be able to survive the worst. Although I didn't want to find out.

Could I share these techniques with others? Maybe as Stephen Cope said in "The Great Work of Your Life" workshop last year, I could "try on" my dream. I could lead mini-workshops, retreats, even coach – eventually morphing it into a full-time gig. What would that look like?

I took a picture of the tarot card, added some text, and posted it as my meme of the day. Then bundled into my long unsexy puffy parka and headed to the cafeteria to grab coffee for the pre-dawn walk to the labyrinth. They provided coffee in the cafeteria now, but the cups were tiny. I finished mine before leaving the building.

The footstep path to the labyrinth was covered with four to five inches of snow. It wound down one hill and up another. As my boots shifted on the uneven terrain, I mused that Mario wouldn't have been able to join me. A walk like this would've been too hard for him.

Maybe I could bring Patrick here for the summer retreat. He's active. A runner even. Then I felt guilty because I loved Patrick and still felt engaged to Mario, and because I loved Mario and was now with Patrick. I wondered when I'd stop feeling like I was cheating on them both.

I reached the archway to the labyrinth and noticed a five-foot pole with the words "May Peace Prevail on Earth" written in different languages on each of its four sides. In the labyrinth, the trail was invisible. Snow had covered everything. The winding path was obliterated, and only the stone altar in the middle remained. Crystals, pennies, and small toy mementos adorned its top, and two shiny kids' windmills were stuck in the snow beside it.

Neither windmill was moving. The air was still. I looked away toward the east and thought of Mario. A year ago I'd heard his voice telling me he was going to the market to get wings for the Super Bowl.

And then - nothing more.

I looked over. One of the windmills stirred, a slow turn. Then it was still like its partner. Did that really happen? Had something or someone made it move?

"Is that you, Mario?" I whispered. The windmill didn't reply. I looked around to see if anyone could see me talking to a toy. No. I was alone – physically. Spiritually though, Mario was with me. Daddy and Mother too.

I noticed the worn teak bench by the maze entrance and sat to wait for the sunrise despite a sky full of clouds. I looked up through the wire-trimmed trellis, toward the lake.

Suddenly my toes were freezing. I looked at my phone to check the time and saw a text from Patrick. "Good morning beautiful." He sent a song link by MFSB. I clicked it and "The Sound of Philadelphia" beckoned me home. If I packed up the car now, I could leave right after the workshop ended and we could watch the Super Bowl together. An appealing thought, except for him cheering on the Patriots. Again.

I sent him a picture of the peace pole by the labyrinth entrance. He texted, "Nice. They have one of those at the kids' school. How're you feeling?"

Looking up, I saw rays of light peeking through the grey clouds hovering over the lake. Even though they obscured the sunrise I texted, "Better…hopeful." Maybe *this* was the peace that passes all understanding.

I rose from the bench and started a new path to the retreat center. No need to wait anymore.

Even though I couldn't see it, the sun had already risen.

# ACKNOWLEDGMENTS

This book has taken six years to complete and covers three years of my life. Most names have been changed out of respect, and to allow folks to tell their own stories - if and when they are ready. And a lighter touch has been given to many characters, mainly because they are minors, or have asked for less focus.

This story started with a twelve-month blog inspired by the memoir *Julie & Julia*. After Mario's death, this little yoga tale became a memoir with the help of both Heather Sellers and Anne Dubuisson. Along the way Jennifer Schelter, Katie Fleming, Cheryl Rice, Matty Dalrymple, and Holly Thomas played supporting roles by writing alongside, mentoring, editing, or serving as honest and kind beta readers. Thank you for all your time and support.

Thank you to my brilliant cover and book designer, Amy Junod Placentra. Your work is beautiful and inspiring - and your patience and creativity tremendous gifts. And thank you to my talented sound engineer Kieran Ferris for patiently guiding and supporting me through the narration for the audio version of the book.

This all wouldn't have happened without my yoga teachers.

From the first (Patty Diamondstone) to the last (Erin Byron), and all those in-between: Bob and Kristen Butera, Colleen Robinson, Lisa Sparta, Libby Piper, Erika Tenenbaum, Julianne Ruocco, Bheem Bhat, Candace Stevens, and Maura Manzo. I am in awe of all of you. Thank you for your part in my yoga journey.

And to my Reiki teacher and psychic Cristina Leeson, thank you for your inspiration and intuition. And for helping me put all the pieces together.

To Stephen Cope, Michael A. Singer, Sharon Salzberg, Brené Brown, and Maria Sirois: your books and workshops healed me in ways I cannot fully express. And to Kripalu – sincere gratitude for providing a sacred space for all us seekers. May you all be happy, healthy, safe, and live with ease.

To all my ele-friends and editors at *Elephant Journal*, thank you for teaching me how to write for the benefit of others. And for giving me a safe place to work on this story, and my voice.

Thank you to all the friends who got me through the years captured in this book and in particular, my divorce mentors Alison Saunders and Sherry Colburn. And of course, thank you to Renee Freilich, the best therapist and friend anyone could have.

To my siblings, thank you for your support and love.

To Joy Hohn who has always been there and loved me no matter what. We are so grateful to have your kind and gentle presence in our lives.

Thank you to Samson, Yogi, and Jake – aka The Wonder Dogs. For understanding how to get me out of my funks, and for loving me even when I forget to take you out or feed you when I'm writing.

Thank you to Mario's family, especially his three amazing

children, and Tony – the best almost-brother-in-law a girl could wish for.

Thank you to Mario – who healed us all with his love and kindness. Thank you for continuing to watch over us and for sending the occasional cardinal or hummingbird when needed.

Thank you to my fellow Musketeers for their patience and love and for being the best children any parent could want or imagine.

And finally, thank you to Patrick, for loving me back to life.

# BOOK CLUB / WORKSHOP QUESTIONS

1.  In the book's opening, Donna thinks Reiki is too "woowoo." How does this change through the course of the story?

2.  How does Donna's relationship with her children change during the book? With Jim? With her mother?

3.  How does yoga help Donna navigate her childhood? Her divorce? Mario's death? Meeting Patrick again?

4.  What are some ways the scenery in the chapters illustrates what is happening in the story?

5.  What are some of the signs or messages that Donna and Sienna get from Mario and others that have passed?

6.  How does Donna's drinking change during the story?

7.  How does the dogs' arrival affect the family?

8.  Do you see any significance in the sunsets and sunrises in the book? The Billy Joel song references?

9.  In what ways does the universe play a role in the story?

10. What is the significance of the title? Is there more than one way it applies?

11. What are some of the missed connections in the book?

12. Did you notice how many references there are to being with people when they die? What is gained by those experiences?

13. What do you think happens to Donna and Patrick after the book's end? Why do you think they found each other again?

# VALUABLE RESOURCES / RECOMMENDED READING

## BOOKS

- *The Pure Heart of Yoga* – Bob Butera
- *Wisdom of Yoga* – Stephen Cope
- *LovingKindness: The Revolutionary Art of Happiness* – Sharon Salzberg
- *A Short Course in Happiness After Loss* – Maria Sirois
- *Radical Acceptance* – Tara Brach
- *Devotions* – Mary Oliver
- *Yoga for the Creative Soul* – Erin Byron
- *The Gifts of Imperfection* – Brene' Brown
- *When Things Fall Apart* – Pema Chodron
- *The Untethered Soul* – Michael Singer
- *Little Book of Bhavana* – Leah Weiss

## MEDITATION APPS

- *Ten Percent Happier*
- *Insight Timer*

## RETREATS / WORKSHOPS

- *Kripalu Yoga Center – www.kripalu.org*
- *The Radiant Retreat – www.jenniferschelter.com*

# WE'VE GOT TO STOP MEETING LIKE THIS PLAYLIST (ON SPOTIFY)

- "Crazy Lucky" – Better Than Ezra
- "True Love" – P!NK
- "Gravity" – Sara Bareilles
- "If I Ever Lose My Faith in You" - Sting
- "Bad Blood" – Taylor Swift
- "Someone New" - Hozier
- "Bust a Move" – Young MC
- "Don't Stop Believin' " – Journey
- "Heartbreak Warfare" – John Mayer
- "New York State of Mind" – Billy Joel
- "Free Fallin'" – Tom Petty
- "Back in the High Life Again" – Steve Winwood
- "Got My Mind Set On You" – George Harrison
- "We'll Be Together" - Sting
- "Singing in the Rain" – Gene Kelly
- "Just the Way You Are" – Billy Joel
- "Like I'm Gonna Lose You" – Meghan Trainor, John Legend
- "Die a Happy Man" – Thomas Rhett
- "Greensleeves" – Vince Guaraldi Trio
- "Only the Good Die Young" – Billy Joel
- "Every Little Thing She Does is Magic" – The Police
- "Daybreak" – Medwyn Goodall
- "Fallen" – Sarah McLachlan
- "Viva La Vida" – Coldplay
- "Point of Know Return" – Kansas
- "Wish You Were Here" – Pink Floyd
- "The Season's Upon Us" – Dropkick Murphys

# ABOUT THE AUTHOR

 **Donna Y. Ferris** lives in West Chester, Pennsylvania with her husband and dogs - and spends as much time as possible with her two Musketeers in Pittsburgh (the home of her beloved Steelers). *We've Got to Stop Meeting Like This* is her first book. Donna continues to work in corporate America and has contributed more than thirty articles to *Elephant Journal.* She also teaches yoga weekly, workshops quarterly, and leads Spring and Fall retreats in Duck, North Carolina. To sign up for Donna's monthly newsletter email her at donnayferris@minichangeyoga.com. You can also follow her on Facebook and Instagram (@downdogdiva) and Twitter (@minidva). If you liked this book please give it a review on Goodreads, Amazon, Barnes & Noble, social media, or anywhere else that might be helpful. Thank you.

Made in the USA
Monee, IL
10 April 2022

94096552R00173